"See Ya Later Shit Lords!"
Mongol Rally 2016

"See Ya Later Shit Lords!" Mongol Rally 2016

Edward Blackwell

Michael Parlby

Edward Blackwell
2017

Copyright © 2017 by Edward Blackwell
All rights reserved. This book or any portion thereof may not be reproduced or used in any manner whatsoever without the express written permission of the publisher except for the use of brief quotations in a book review or scholarly journal.

First Printing: 2017

ISBN 978-1-326-98301-7

Edward Blackwell
Crofts Cottage, Darley
Liskeard, Cornwall. PL14 5AS

www.bataarlatethannever.com
www.facebook.com/bataarlatethannever

Dedication

This book is dedicated to
Mikey
Without whom this adventure would not have been possible. (Actually it might have been easier without all the flat tyres).
"You can be my wingman any time".

Also to Henry and Frosty.
Thanks for an amazing convoy, and sticking with us right up until the Pug gave up.

Finally to all Family, Friends, and Sponsors who supported us through it all.

Contents

Foreword xi
Preface xiii
Introduction 1
Chapter 1: Welcome along to the First Blog 3
Chapter 2: The Difficult Second Blog 6
Chapter 3: The Day of Reckoning has arrived 9
Chapter 4: The Adventure Begins 11
Chapter 5: The Launch 13
Chapter 6: Ferry Antics 15
Chapter 7: Heidelberg Convoy 19
Chapter 8: The Perfect Spot 21
Chapter 9: Hungarian Hunk 24
Chapter 10: Rila Lake Regret 27
Chapter 11: Black Sea Sunrise 31
Chapter 12: Birthday Bonanza 33
Chapter 13: Getting Air in Asia 37
Chapter 14: Kebabs and Tyres 39
Chapter 15: Border Boredom 42
Chapter 16: Tbilisi Baths 44
Chapter 17: Lucky Escape 46
Chapter 18: Park Anywhere 49
Chapter 19: Still in Baku 52

Chapter 20: Still No Sign of Ferry 54

Chapter 21: Hotel Chuck-a-left..56

Chapter 22: See Ya Later Shit Lords 58

Chapter 23: Turkmenistan Torment..61

Chapter 24: Ashgabat and Door to Hell 65

Chapter 25: A Bad Day All Round 70

Chapter 26: Benzene and Tyres...73

Chapter 27: Not the Best 48 Hours 75

Chapter 28: Pamir Highway..78

Chapter 29: Pamir Problems 81

Chapter 30: Out of the Frying Pan into the Fire.............84

Chapter 31: "Dollar" 88

Chapter 32: MISHA...91

Chapter 33: All Nighter 95

Chapter 34: Road to Russia 98

Chapter 35: Mother Russia... 101

Chapter 36: "Fifty Bucks" 103

Chapter 37: She Lives!! 106

Chapter 38: The Final Curtain 110

Chapter 39: Officially Finished 113

Chapter 40: Dominique's Eulogy 116

Epilogue.. 120

Appendix i: The Charities 124

Appendix ii: The Sponsors.. 127

Appendix iii: Dos and Don'ts 130
Appendix iv: The Route 132
Appendix v: Kit List 134
Appendix vi: Currency Conversions 141

Foreword

Just like all good friendships start, I met Ed the author in a bar with his best mate Mikey. Though unlike most friendships, this bar was in Istanbul, during a military coup, after driving a 15-year-old French car called Puggles across Europe with my oppo', Frosty. Sadly, Puggles didn't make it to Mongolia, for circumstances that will become clear later. Still, the four of us enjoyed each other's company and stuck together for the greatest summer I've ever had. This book is the story about that summer from the point of view of a 22-year-old engineering graduate from Cornwall, whom I believe to be downright insane.

You start to question the sanity of a person who chooses to drive 15 hours a day, every day, over 40 days. You really start to question it, when the person chooses to drive across the largest supercontinent in an 800cc Daewoo Matiz with one pair of flip flops and 5 T-shirts (And then travel around India in the same honking rig)!

However, I realised the author of this book was truly off his rocker when after driving 600km at night, on roads last resurfaced around the time of Christ, with 10 hours sleep in the last 5 days, he erected his hammock in the middle of literally nowhere, made himself a cup of tea and began to blog (Köneürgenç, Turkmenistan to be more exact). He blogged every night, without fail. No matter how many breakdowns, borders, burglaries or beers that had occurred the day before, he wouldn't sleep without blogging. The daily exhaustion and sporadic shit you face when attempting to complete what Ed and Mikey achieved in the timescale they did is remarkable - especially when you consider the vehicle of choice. I was once told that the distance between insanity and genius is measured only by a person's success. So, I guess the fact their efforts have been transformed into a book suggests they weren't that nuts after all…

Senseless or not. I can now confirm that the two men in this story were fundamental to what I will look back on as the defining summer of my life. My biggest concern before the rally was failing to meet new people to share this unbelievable experience with. People I would genuinely consider friends in the 'real world', a world outside of tiny cars and random bars. Fortunately for myself and Frosty, we managed to form a very strong friendship with two of the most genuine, loyal and selfless people I have ever met.

There is a specific type of person who attempts the Mongol Rally, Ed and Mikey completely personify that ethos. They made the hard times bearable and the good times unforgettable. By sheer luck, they managed to plan a rally which ticked every box you'd want to tick, making this the perfect book for anyone wishing to attempt this adventure. The book was written in situ, giving a primary and emotive account through 40 days of life changing mayhem.

I hope if you're reading this, you're also the type of person that would attempt the Rally. Even though mine ended in tears, I wouldn't swap the experience for the world and I would do it again in a heartbeat. I urge all readers to seriously consider the Mongol Rally and I am sure this book will do nothing but motivate you to give it a go! I just hope you're lucky enough to meet people of the magnitude that Ed, Mikey and of course Frosty are - you will be just as lucky as I was. They're friends for life and I will never forget the stories we created in two crappy cars in the middle of fucking nowhere.

Henry McCann
March 2017

Preface

Before you read any further I want to warn you that this isn't the next Michael Palin travel thriller, nor is it the next Game of Thrones, for a start there are no dragons, or tits. In fact there are two tits in this story, they will be taking it in turns to drive the red car.

And if you think this is one of those books about how we went to go and find ourselves in Asia, on our Gap Year, with mummy's bank card, then think again. Put the book back on the Waterstone's shelf, in the number one bestseller's position, and kindly exit the store.

However, if you don't like Wizards or Dragons and want to find out how two school friends, from the West Country, fared on their quest, then please continue to read on.

This book is a collection of the blogs I wrote every day whilst I was undertaking the Mongol Rally, with Mikey and Dominique in the summer of 2016. I like to think these blogs were a frank and truthful account, with no hidden agenda (other than to raise as much money as possible), of what it is like to spend five weeks on the road in a tiny red car.

To set the scene, I would write these sat in the passenger seat during Mikey's driving stint. The passenger was also responsible for being the DJ, Navigator, and official scribe for the many competition charts Mikey and I had between us. I took great pleasure in marking up every one of Mikey's nine flat tyres, only to realise we didn't have the Uzbek AA on standby and we were the only ones that were going to change it.

I wanted to collate the entries into some sort of memory for myself, mainly. It will also give those of you that were following our story as it happened, a chance to find out the ending to our adventure, as I know the website decided it wasn't going to upload anymore blog entries after Turkmenistan. (Spoiler alert we survived).

Anyway, I have tried to keep the blogs as the original entries as much as possible, but there might be a few spelling corrections, explanations, and addition snippets of information that I have slotted in as footnotes. I did not know these facts at the time, but I thought they would be of interest.

This book is being published by Lulu.com and sold on their website as well as amazon. The publishing is free but this means the corporate monkey takes a sizeable chunk of your hard earned money you used to buy this book. The small portion left goes to me and I will be donating all the proceeds I receive to our rally charities. (More information on each charity in the Appendices at the end of the book). That means you can enjoy this book knowing that at least something is going to help others.

I hope you enjoy this as much as I enjoyed collecting the information for the book.

"See Ya Later Shit Lords!"

Introduction

The Mongol Rally is a car rally that begins in Europe and originally ended in Ulan Bataar, Mongolia. To avoid punitive costs and taxes associated with vehicle imports and disposal, the rally now passes through Mongolia and ends in Ulan Ude, Russia. The principal launch is from London, United Kingdom, with subsidiary starting points in the Czech Republic. It is described as the "greatest adventure in the world". There are three fundamental Rules of the Rally:

The car must be small and rubbish.

Teams are totally unsupported.

Teams need to raise at least £1000 for charity.

The rally is designed to be an adventure for the participants, and not a traditional rally/race. The organisers ("The Adventurists") are careful to point out that racing on highways is illegal, and that no recognition is given to the first finisher. There are other differences from mainstream rallies, particularly the fact that no support team is provided and no other arrangements are made such as for accommodation. Indeed, the diminutive vehicles are deliberately inappropriate for the task, in the adventurous spirit of the rally.

The inaugural rally took place in 2004, in which 6 teams started and 4 completed the course. The second rally, in 2005, was entered by 43 teams, and 18 automobiles arrived intact in Ulan Bataar. The 2006 Rally began on July 22 with 167 cars setting off. 117 teams made it to Ulan Bataar.

The Mongol Rally was run as a charity event from 2004 to 2006 with all of the proceeds from the entry fees used to organise the event with the remaining donated to charity. This changed from 2007 as the event is now organised by the League of Adventurists International Ltd, a privately owned profit making UK company. However, the participants continue to raise money for charities through sponsorship.

"See Ya Later Shit Lords!"

The 2007 rally left Hyde Park, London, on 21 July and was limited to 200 teams. Registration for 2007 was far more popular than the organisers could have foreseen, with the first 100 places allocated in 22 seconds. Due to this popularity, the final 50 places were awarded on the result of a ballot. In 2007, places were awarded for 2008 in two sign ups with places assigned on 1 November and 7 November. The entry fee was £650 per team. The main British starting point moved from Hyde Park, London, to Goodwood in West Sussex for the 2009 to 2012 events. Cars lapped the circuit in procession before departing. In 2013 the launch was from Bodiam Castle in Sussex and in 2014 it returned to London, launching from Battersea Park.

This information was taken from Wikipedia, if you are interested in taking part you can sign up at the link below. The next place to look is AutoTrader to start choosing your chariot. If all this hasn't whetted your appetite, read on and immerse yourself in the experiences Mikey and I had in the summer of 2016.

www.theadventurists.com/mongol-rally

"See Ya Later Shit Lords!"

Chapter 1: Welcome along to the First Blog

03 Jul 2016

I am sat on a train, hungover, heading back to Leeds to pick up the car that will be our mode of transport, and home, for the 5 weeks of Mongol Rally. I thought this would be the perfect time to kick off the blog writing with two weeks to go before Mikey and I embark on our adventure of a lifetime.

I will give you a brief back story of what the Rally is all about, but I feel as if you have got this far you will already have a pretty good idea as to what is involved. The basic idea is to drive a car from the Goodwood Motor Circuit, near London, to Ulan Ude in Russia, which is approximately 10,000 miles. I hear you saying "That doesn't sound too difficult". I would have agreed with you until I let you know that the car has to have an engine size of less than 1 litre, and is preferably a shit heap.

The description above could not be more apt for the 0.8 litre Daewoo Matiz we ended up buying for £300. I naively (and stupidly after just completely a degree in engineering) thought a car this cheap would get the job done. Just a quick road trip to Mongolia. Nothing to worry about. I could not have been more wrong. A list as long as your arms and legs, which I still don't know the full extent (more details to follow), has been trickled back to me. We gave the car to John 'Xzibit' Earp, a mechanically minded friend of my girlfriends family, for 'a once over' and an MOT. We are both extremely grateful to John for making sure the car will actually reach, what is now, Europe after the recent 'Brexit' activities. My arrival back in Leeds will be the first time I will have seen our ride after its recent pimpin'.

I am travelling back from a school reunion (of sorts) and this was the second time Mikey and I have actually seen each other, in person, since we decided to take on this colossal challenge (obviously we have been friends since school, for those that don't know us and happened upon this blog because it is more of a viral sensation than Kim Kardashian's arse). The first, in person, meet up was our unsuccessful trip to the Russian visa application centre in Manchester. We had spent the previous week ensuring all the various paperwork was in order, as they have been known to be extremely meticulous. Despite this, I thought our visit was going to uneventful and we would be in and out, swiftly. However, as previous evidence suggest my expectations need re-evaluating, as no sooner had we handed over our paperwork, confident everything was correct, it was back in our hands. There was no email on the application. The application was completed by the Visa Machine, who hold the password, therefore rendering it un-editable. This turned out to be the least of our worries, as we mentioned in passing that we doing the Mongol Rally, a game changer in the eyes of the Russian visa guy.

The short story is, we were told we had the completely wrong visas and if we turned up to the border with this type of visa we were going to have to complete our trip on horseback. As neither Mikey, nor I, have experiences with horses this was going to be a show stopper. After worriedly ringing the visa machine, they assured us that these were the correct type of visas and people had been completing the rally on these for the past 10 years. They had failed to mention to us that we were not meant to disclose what we were doing on our trip to Russia.

All is not lost though. We have a second chance at trying to obtain the allusive Russian visa, this time in London. We are going next week, and is just one of the many things on our 'To Do List' before we leave to drive over a third of the world. We will be sure there is no mention of the rally. I was toying with the idea of using a cover story as a couple looking for a romantic getaway to Ulan Ude, but I have a feeling that will go down worse than the well-known atrocity of DRIVING A CAR ACROSS THE COUNTRY.

This is taking maximum priority on 'The List' at the moment, but we are under no illusions that there is a lot to do in the two weeks before we make our way to Goodwood. I wanted to capture how I felt at this moment, knowing that there are no other distractions and the full focus is on preparation. It's the same feeling of excitement

"See Ya Later Shit Lords!"

mixed with apprehensive that I experienced when we first confirmed our registration on this adventure and when I first picked up the car from Durham (it was a surprise she made it to Leeds, knowing what we do now). It's a great feeling to have and I know it will become greater as the start date draws nearer.

I think that is enough for a first blog. We will try our best to update this blog (and the other social media outputs) daily, whilst we are away, and there will probably a couple more in the next two weeks letting you know how the prep is going and the outcome of the Russian visa application. I invite you to stay tuned to find out how two friends from the South West fare in the big wide world. I already think of you, the reader, as the third member of our team. Go on, make yourself comfortable on the backseat, put your seat belt on though, because it's going to be one hell of a ride!

Chapter 2: The Difficult Second Blog

10 Jul 2016

Here it is then, the highly anticipated difficult second blog. I am once again hungover writing this blog (I hope this does not become a regular theme), I am watching the tennis reflecting on the week that has passed since the last blog. A lot has happened, but there is still a lot to do in this coming week before we set the, skateboard sized, wheels of the Matiz rolling around the Goodwood Motor Circuit.

The first main news is that we have the pimped up car back from Rawcliffe Motors. The work completed on the car is not obvious from the outside, other than the bolted on roof bars, but trust me her insides have had more work done than Katie Price. The list includes new: clutch, brakes, windscreen wipers, exhaust sensors, and lots more that I can't remember at this moment in time. What is important, is that the car now runs like a dream (other than a slight knocking nose over 50mph), and has made it all the way down from Leeds to Cornwall. I know this distance is nothing compared to what we have to cover, but it is a start.

It was last Tuesday when I drove down from Leeds, there was a quick detour for Mikey and I to meet up, in London, to sort out the final hurdle in terms of visas, the notorious Russian Visa. We were both expecting the worst as we met on Gee Street, we didn't go in to the Visa Application Centre until we had our story straight, as to why we were visiting Russia and to agree that the Rally would not be mentioned once we were over the threshold, otherwise it would be curtains. However, a quick frisk by the Russian security guard (who looked suspiciously like Jaws from James Bond, or is that my prejudices of Russians creeping in? I might keep that to myself when we cross the border), meant we could collect a ticket and queue to submit our application. You are probably thinking that we were waiting there for hours, days, weeks, and that we have only just got home today, but we were in and out relatively quickly, without being

"See Ya Later Shit Lords!"

quizzed on the reasons for visiting. This Tuesday is the day of reckoning, and when we will know whether the visa has been accepted or not. If successful, our passports will be posted to us by Thursday. Which is cutting it rather close, but I faith in the Russians.

This trip down to Devon/Cornwall was also Mikey's first encounter with our South Korean Whip. His initial reactions were, and I quote, "it's a lot smaller than I expected" which is a statement that I'm sure Mikey is more used to hearing rather than actually saying himself. After getting over the shock of realising that he would be spending the best part of five weeks in this roller skate, Mikey was impressed with the performance and handling of the little red devil (until we got to a gentle incline).

With the car now down in Devon, it gave us a chance to do our own work on the car. I'm afraid to admit reader, but that comfy backseat that I promised you in the last blog, to allow you to join us on our adventure, is now a thing of history. We have ditched them to save weight and to give us more room for activities/luggage. We have traded the weight of the seats for a roof box, and you are more than welcome to stow away in there for the trip.

Other work has included taking the trim off the car and PAINTING THE WALLS OF THE TYRES WHITE. I hear those of you that have not seen any mafia films asking, "Will this stop them from getting a punctures?" and "Will it improve the performance of the car?" The answer is no. White walled tyres have no effect, other than on the ladies. In fact the work that Mikey and I have done on the car has had no, if not a negative, effect on the performance of the car.

As you can imagine, there is still a lot to do in the week before we leave. The first of which is a lesson on general car maintenance from Mikey's local mechanic friend, Keith Richards (no not that one). Hopefully Keith will be able to teach us to know our arses from our elbows (or our tail-lights from our universal joints), to give us a fighting chance of being able to get the car to a local mechanic should we break down. But I don't see it happening, we are only driving 10,000 miles, over a third of the world, in a 14 year old shit heap. What could go wrong?

Other things to consider before we leave, make sure we have all the kit ready to be packed up on Friday, get in contact with our sponsors to say our final thank you's and farewells, attach all the sponsor's stickers, and finally mentally prepare ourselves for the trip ahead. That strange feeling that I mentioned in last week's blog, of excitement and apprehension, is still here and is particularly prominent today. Or that might be the 12 ales from last night's Beer festival trying to make a comeback.

I think that is enough for this week, I will write another instalment before we set off for Goodwood on Saturday. It will let you know how the week of preparation has gone, whether the feeling was excitement or vomit, and how far up the scale of "one to fucked" we are. I hope that is enough of a teaser to see you here again on Friday!

"See Ya Later Shit Lords!"

Chapter 3: The Day of Reckoning has arrived

15 Jul 2016

You will be pleased to know that I am not actually hungover whilst writing this blog (fans of the previous blog, "The Difficult Second Blog", will also be pleased to know that it was excitement I was feeling and the 12 ales did not reappear), however a sobering thought for anyone is the realisation that you have to pack everything you may need to you get you to Russia, in the next five weeks, in a car that is barley bigger than a child's shoe and has less power than Ed Miliband.

This is going to be a brief blog, as it is late after a long day of final preparations. But I want to get you up to speed with what has been happening since Sunday. And, my oh my, a lot has happened indeed.

On Monday we had our lesson from Keith Richards (not that one!!!!). He, and Simon, were extremely helpful in showing us where everything was on the car and the various problems we may face. This daunting list prompted an order of a number of spare parts, which were picked up, and packed, immediately. One of the many questions we had for our mechanically gifted friends was the mysterious knocking/beeping noise that the car was making on the rare occasion it reached over 50mph. We took Simon out for a spin to see if he could diagnose what it might be. He reckoned it was something to do with the fan belt, but assured us it would be fine. It's strange, because when you turn the music up louder it seems to disappear. My own diagnosis is not quite complete, but I'm sure the two are linked. We will keep you updated, of course.

The rest of the week involved a sporadic shopping trip, lasting about three days. We made list after list, but still we were thinking of things that we may need. Amazon orders were made, with the delivery cost becoming more expensive by the day. We visited various

"See Ya Later Shit Lords!"

breakers yards to find some skateboard sized spare wheels. Eventually we got to today which was when the sponsorship stickers finally arrived, and the time for packing was upon us.

I will give you a quick list of our sponsors, and I hope to go into more detail in future blogs.[1]

Gold: Fletcher's Solicitors

Silver: Milford Farm, Rotary International, Graspan Frankton

Bronze: GoFilmYourself, Polyflor, Advanced engravers

These have all been immortalised in sticker form and are now decorating the car, as they say 'a picture paints a thousand words'. Enjoy.[2]

Welcome back, there isn't a huge amount more to say, I apologise for the lack of interesting content in this blog, but this reflects how we have been feeling. We need to get all the boring preparation and paperwork so we can get to the good stuff. So hopefully the blog will pick up in line with us setting off on this adventure. I want to leave you with the thought below.

Back in January, when we first signed up to undertake this huge challenge, tomorrow was a day that was very much 'future' Ed and Mikey's problem to deal with, and something that we would never thought would actually materialise. But now that the last day of preparation has come and gone, it has now dawned on us that tomorrow is the start of the unknown. Planning and preparation stops. Adventure begins.

---

[1] I never actually went into further detail in future blogs, but if the advertising has worked on you and you want to know more about any of our sponsors, go to the Appendices at the back of the book, the bit you'll probably skip at the end.

[2] Go to facebook.com/bataarlatethannever for the pictures.

"See Ya Later Shit Lords!"

Chapter 4: The Adventure Begins

16 Jul 2016

Last night I lay awake thinking about the trip we have ahead of us. The What If's, the have we over packed (which I'm certain we most definitely have), the How are we going to drive this car 10,000 miles?

The first bit of good news is that we have christened the car, "Dominique". We thought about this long and hard and feel as if "Dominique the Daewoo" has a certain ring to it and rolls off the tongue nicely. From now on our trusty stead will be referred to as Dominique, so if you have joined the blog late, it is not some Eastern European stripper that has stowed herself in the roofbox. Whilst we are on the roofbox subject I just wanted to let all of those Car-Packing fans know that the roofbox we have chosen has turned out to be some sort of Tardis. It is just unbelievable how much that plastic coffin can fit inside it. More updates on the roofbox to follow.

As interesting as the capacity of the roofbox is, I'm sure you came to this blog hoping to find out how those Crazy Cats, Mikey and Ed, are getting on during their first day of driving.

Spirits were high, this morning, as we finally finished packing our last bits into the car and had our various sponsorship photos with the car. And that was it, we said our goodbyes to Mikey's family and set off for Goodwood. That feeling of excitement and apprehension was now replaced with a kind of emptiness. The preparation was over, we were now actually doing it. It wasn't that we didn't want to get to this stage, it was what we had been planning for the past 6 months, and it was just that the realisation hadn't sunk in yet. It felt as if we were going for a drive. This was most prominent when, at the end of my final Skype call with my parents, my Dad says 'Oh text us when you get to Mongolia', as if we were just driving down the road to a mates house. In some ways we are just driving, but this is a big deal, an experience of a lifetime.

"See Ya Later Shit Lords!"

Three Hours into our journey, Mikey has already left the cash machine without taking his money, we have forgotten a lead for the GoPro which means we can't charge one of them, and there is a persistent fuel leak, when we fill the tank all the way to the top, even though an expert repair job with Duct Tape was undertaken. Anyway things could be worse.

We have just seen our first other Mongol Rally team. We gave them a flash, with the new spotlights we fitted ourselves (not our penises). I'm surprised they are not now blind, as the lights could be described as a couple of Night Sun's.

We are now just arriving, so we will reconvene tomorrow, where I am certain to be hungover again after the launch party.

"See Ya Later Shit Lords!"
Chapter 5: The Launch

17 Jul 2016

We are now on the ferry to Dunkirk, tucking into a nice curry and a beer, after a morning of festivities at the launch of the Rally, followed by a cruise down to Dover.

I started the day, waking up in our tent (which is not going to be our permanent sleeping arrangement, we have hammocks to use, but there was nowhere to string them in the open field that was the campsite. So thank you to both Mikey's mum, and the new Tesco in Tavistock, for insisting that we take it. You were right.), extremely early and hungover (surprise) from the pre-launch party booze up. This was where we met our first friends on the rally, the Kiwi team 'Puncture, What Puncture?'. They set up camp next to our tents and noticed that one of their team and myself share a last name, this was the ice breaker for the evening. We quickly set up our camping chairs in a sociable circle, beers in the arm holsters and we settled down for a night of drinking warm beverages and story swapping.

I went to retrieve the car from her overnight paddock, or as I like to think of it, an orgy of shitty little cars. Dominique looked like she had enjoyed herself last night. We packed up our stuff, and drove over to another holding paddock ready to do our lap of the Goodwood circuit. This was something I had been looking forward to since we signed up. I wanted to see what Dominique had to offer in terms of lap times and sector splits, the record for Goowood is 59 seconds, I wanted to get close. (SPOILER ALERT - we didn't.)

Before this long awaited lap, and start of our adventure, there was about a two hour wait. This included an awards ceremony and some traditional Mongolian wrestlers showing how scary they could be if you ploughed through a Yurt in your hatchback. This interlude also allowed us to meet up with Mikey's family one last time, they had brought the GoPro lead that I had forgotten, as well as Mikey's literature for the trip. This exchange of books led to the most Public

"See Ya Later Shit Lords!"

School sentence I have ever heard. Mikey pipes up after having discovered what books were in the bag "Who the fuck put Conan-Doyle in here, I just wanted Hemmingway!"

With Hemmingway securely packed (and Doyle left firmly in the bag), it was finally time to do our lap and leave on our epic adventure. We lined up at the back of the starting grid, coincidentally behind our kiwi friends from the night before. All that feeling of emptiness and apprehension had disappeared, all that was present was excitement and adrenaline, and plenty of it. When our time came I dropped the clutch and hit the accelerator pedal hard, we set off at a moderately average rate of knots, but our speed was gaining. Everyone was sort of sticking one behind each other in a boring snake-like fashion, but I was having none of that. I was practicing for the Nurburgring. I razzed it past the kiwis, and didn't stop there. I felt like I was Lewis Hamilton, but with a massively top heavy car (something Lewis would not be pleased about), I wasn't getting the response from the car that I wanted. It felt as if she could tip any time as I chucked her into the corners. This didn't stop me from weaving in and out of traffic. This was a land where there were no rules, this was the Mongol Rally. It felt absolutely awesome.

After the adrenaline fuelled lap was over, it was then time to drive to Dover to catch the ferry we are on now. It had finally sunk in, we were doing the Mongol rally, no more weird feelings. It just felt right. The anonymous, forgettable, British motorways and A-roads to Dover were nothing to write home about, but it obviously had to be done. However, it did give us chance to tweak a few home comforts in the car.

We are just about to dock in Dunkirk, we have left the UK, and heading for the EU (still too soon?). Our plan is to head to a wooded area just outside Brussels, so we can use our hammocks for the first time. Were we arrested for being homeless? Find out in the next blog.

"See Ya Later Shit Lords!"

Chapter 6: Ferry Antics

18 Jul 2016

I'll try and pick up from where I left off when we were on the ferry, from yesterday, I believe we were just about to dock. We were disembarking from the ferry, when the guys from team 'Gold Member' asked us what our route was, they were planning on heading the same way so we decided to convoy once we were off.

This did not go as well as we had planned, even though we had our nifty radios, we had lost the others in an instance. We cruised off on our own from Dunkirk, after the brief 30 second convoy had formed, the French countryside very quickly became the Belgian. We needed to stop for fuel (this is going to be an all too frequent sentence, due to the Ribena sized fuel tank, which also has a leak). Once we had got accustom to the Belgian fuel filling system we set off again for some woodland, just south of Brussels, to string up our hammocks.

On our way down, we spotted the gold Fiat Panda in convoy with the Irish team, 'Aristokhans', we shouted on the radio for them to follow us, as I was confident I knew where we were headed. I was wrong. We ended up in suburban Belgium. You only get lost once on the rally. That sounds right, doesn't it? Anyway the 'gold member' team finally got us to the promise land of 'The Woods'.

The spot was perfect. I jumped out of the car, excited to see where we could put the hammocks. I immediately stepped, barefoot, on a slug (the worst feeling in the world, after putting your socks on in the morning), and then I was stung by nettles about a thousand times on the lower leg. The hammocks were erected several times, we had to turn the car side on. The handbrake could not hold both Mikey and myself (mainly Mikey) when the hammocks were attached with the car facing front on. We had discovered this during an unnerving moment when we both sat down triumphantly, and the car started rolling towards us. Finally with the hammocks in the correct positions we settled in for the night.

"See Ya Later Shit Lords!"

I was awoken with a cheerful Belgian park ranger wiggling my toes, he politely told us that we weren't allowed to camp here, but we could take as much time as we wanted to clear off. A nice start to the day.

Today was all about the Nurburgring, but first we split off from the convoy to check out what Brussels had to offer. Not much it turns out, apart from a decent traditional Belgian breakfast and, by far, the worst public toilets I have ever experienced. I won't go into too much detail, but all I will say is: brown lake and log.

We quickly left the Belgian capital behind and headed for the Nurburgring, whilst looking for a river to wash ourselves. The Netherlands, although we were there for a short amount of time, provided this delight. We pulled up at a murky river and asked some locals if we could swim, they said no and suggested what sounded like 'Grinder', which I now thinking is a lake of some sort. We insisted we weren't a couple and moved on to the next small Dutch village, this had the perfect river, we jumped straight in and washed away happily. No more 'Whores baths/student showers' for us.

Feeling like new men, we continued to Nurburg. We pulled up at what we thought was the public track, only for a nice German gentleman to tell us that Dominique would not be going round the circuit. It turned out to be the F1 track, however we were pointed in the direction of the famous public track. This was after I schooled Mikey at indoor go karting. I have the sheet of lap times to prove it, I'm hiding it until I have a chance to securely fix it to the car to make sure Mikey never forgets.

The Nurburgring experience was like nothing I have felt before. We had to take the roofbox off, which was a good job as we definitely would have rolled Dominique. There were cars coming at us from all angles. Words can't really explain it, and the video doesn't really do it justice either. But I can assure you, it was terrifying. But an awesome rush at the same time. My hands were shaking for a good half an hour afterwards.

"See Ya Later Shit Lords!"

I think my favourite moment from the terrifying lap was when we reached the famous 'Carousel' corner. For those that don't know, it is a hairpin corner that has a severely banked apex to allow cars to accelerate as they swoop round the switchback to ensure quick lap times. It is most certainly not for small shitty Mongol rally cars.

We found out when we returned to the holding area, every other Rally car had stuck to the outside of the track, making sure they didn't get in the way of the serious supercars. However, I did not. I slipped Dominique into second, dropped into the apex, shouting 'I paid my money the same as you', with a queue of about five cars behind me, all flashing and honking, there was no way I was going to miss this opportunity to drive on this iconic corner. There were many gestures and even more honking as I eventually moved out of the way after the corner had finished.

The stream of cars passing us was becoming an all to familiar sight as we neared the end of the lap. However, Mikey and I both new Dominique had an 'overtake' in her. We weren't wrong. After cresting over one of the many hills, our victim was locked in our sights. A brown, clapped out, Volkswagen Passat. Dominique wanted this scalp, I just allowed her. We both knew when the moment was right, on a downhill section, with the wind behind us. As we drew level, the rev counter would have been at the limiter if there had been one, but Dominique pushed onwards. We had our claim to fame. An 'overtake' on the Nurburgring. (We just don't have to mention the car in question).

Finally, all too soon the lap was over. The marshal woman was very shocked to see that we had actually made it back. I think she had the recovery vehicle on standby as we lined up at the start barriers.[3] We purchased one of those douchebag stickers to prove we have done it.

---

[3] The recovery vehicle was in fact needed whilst we were at the track. Just ten minutes after we had successfully negotiated our hot lap, there was an announcement over the loudspeaker. The track was closed due to a crash. We

"See Ya Later Shit Lords!"

We have now joined back up with the Irish team and we are following an Aussie team down to Heidelberg, for the first of the pit stops en route. We are armed with 5% German 1 litre beer cans, purchased and the petrol station. I will let you know how we get on.

didn't know, until we looked it up later on the internet, it was the new Koenigsegg One. The driver had binned it on one of the many twisting corners during its first ever test lap of the Nurburgring. I am just very glad that the Koenigsegg wasn't on the track ten minutes earlier, otherwise we most certainly would have been involved in the £4 million accident.

Chapter 7: Heidelberg Convoy

19 Jul 2016

The convoy down to Heidelberg was fairly uneventful, we followed the Aussie team, who turned out to be kiwis (classic mistake), with the Irish guys behind us. The German autobahn is not all it is cracked up to be, especially when you are in a shit car, it is just as dull as the British motorways. We therefore had to make our own entertainment. This was achieved by filming each other's cars whilst overtaking. Kieran and Steven from the Irish team had some particularly novel poses every time we passed them, these included flashing arses (very original) and gorilla and chicken heads obviously pre-packed for such an eventuality.

We took over the duty of leading the convoy to the first pit stop, after we had stopped to fill up with fuel, yet again. We did discover that the German service stations are much better than ours, this is proved by the fact that you can buy a litre of 5% beer for €2.

We eventually arrived in to Heidelberg at around 2200, and Mikey and I immediately cracked open our bucket sized beers and went to find somewhere to hang our hammocks. We came across a guy called Felix who had had the same idea as us. His hammock was much more advanced than ours, by a long way. It had guy ropes, a mosquito net and special ways to help to create the best type of tension. Ours seemed like something you'd buy from the Early Learning Centre, in comparison, but the main thing was that it kept us away from the horrible slugs.

After finding a spot, we went in search of something to eat, we got the last two pizzas on offer, and were warned about how spicy they were. I don't know whether Germans have different taste buds from us, but this pizza was the mildest thing I have tasted. Maybe that's what makes the British spirit so formidable. Two world wars, and one World Cup, eh.

"See Ya Later Shit Lords!"

Enough of the historical jokes, the Germans have been, the friendliest people we have met so far. Apart from our Belgian park ranger friend. We retired to our sleeping quarters after drinking our comically oversized beers.

Another great night's sleep in the 'Love Hammocks" (as they now shall be known), meant we were feeling refreshed for our drive to a lake just outside Salzburg. We convoyed with Kieran and Steven to Munich, where they had to get their Carnet de Passage for entry into Iran. The most exciting thing to happen was when we joined the very first autobahn, this morning. We trying to get on from the slip road, but the Lorry drivers were having none of it. They were honking and flashing us. Kieran had our back. He chased the main culprit in his faster Ford Fiesta, honking his horn and giving him the finger. This provoked the Lorry man behind us, he proceeded to position his Lorry closer than I would have liked to our bumper. I think he saw our Nurburgring sticker and knew weren't to be messed with, and quickly back off.

The only other news on this section of driving is that we have lost power steering, the belt has completely disappeared, along with the noise it was making before. We had got used to drowning out the noise with the music and opening the windows. The latter is a necessity at all times due to the air con being equivalent to an asthmatic coughing on you after trying to walk up a gentle slope. Hopefully we will be able to pick up a belt somewhere en route to Budapest.

We are just on the outskirts of Salzburg as I write this now. Kieran and Steven, our NBF's (New Best Friends), have just left us. We have exchanged details, so hopefully we will be able to catch up with them in Budapest. There are some beautiful views of the Alps, which is a welcome break from the boring autobahn. I will update you with a review of the lake tomorrow.

"See Ya Later Shit Lords!"
Chapter 8: The Perfect Spot

20 Jul 2016

We pushed on past Salzburg and the eagles nest (Hitler's house in the south of Germany) we wanted to visit both of these places but the desire to set up camp before 2200, as had happened the previous two nights, was greater than our sightseeing needs.

Mikey had read a travellers blog, who promised fantastic camping spots throughout Austria and they were all free. We chose Gause national park as the place we were aiming to pitch our hammocks. Just outside Heiflau we stopped in a town to get some beers for our evening ahead. I was searching for my wash bag, as this is where I had cleverly hidden most of my money. But I was not as clever as I had first thought. In fact I was probably the stupidest person in the car, at that moment. I had left my wash bag on the roof of the car after cleaning my teeth before we left Heidelberg. I must not have noticed it when we set off. Anyway we were now in rural Austria, four hours away. I had resided myself to the fact that had lost most of the money I had budgeted for the trip. I posted on the rally Facebook group, in the hope that some fellow rallier was kind enough to have picked it up. I wasn't holding out too much hope.

However, I was in luck. Someone had already posted a picture of it as lost property. I swiftly made contact, arranging to pick it up in Budapest, the next pit stop. I love the ralliers. I was so relieved.

With my frown turned upside down, Mikey went and purchased some beers for our evening and we set off in search of our camp for the night. The road from 'Washbag gait village' (as I can't remember what it was actually called) was absolutely stunning. We were surrounded by mountains on either side, with the river weaving side to side underneath us, as we ducked momentarily in and out of tunnels. It was idyllic. We had specific needs for a campsite. It had to be near the river but still secluded, as well as being somewhere we could hang our hammocks. We kept on going past Heiflau, looking for the perfect spot. Many places were turned down in the knowing that there must be the perfect place in this spectacular region of Austria just around the next corner. We were hoping this wasn't a classic case of the 'grass being greener' and we'd end up driving to Slovenia.

Then there it was, a little bridge over the much calmer waters which had subsided from the rapids they had once been further up. The bridge led to a lane with many signs in German which we did not know the meaning. We took them to mean 'perfect camping spot' and parked close to the woods and ventured in. What we found was a wooded area on the inside bend of a meander in the river. It was what we had been searching for, and more. We unpacked everything from the car and set up our sleeping quarters for the night. A wash in the river was in order before our 'Boil in the Bag' dinner.

The river was beyond cold, but refreshing at the same time. We washed off the dirt that seems to accumulate whilst sitting in a hot car all day, at what seemed lightening pace. Top tip for anyone washing naked in a freezing cold, fast flowing, river. Do not at any point turn your back upstream. You will be sure to get a cold surprise. That's all I am saying.

The sub-zero enema was soon a thing of the past as we set about lighting a fire. We opened our ice cold beers that had been chilling in the river, cooked and ate the Boil-in-the-Bag delights and tucked ourselves into our hanging beds for another night's sleep.

Sammy slug, had decided to curl up on my flip flops this time. He was gently removed with the flick of a stick and then we set about packing up the camp. We had got up early because we wanted to head down to a waterfall at a national park in Croatia. We would then head across to Budapest for the second pit stop, and to retrieve my wash bag. However, as we were nearing the Slovenian border the car started to make more of a shaking than we were used to. It was time to get it checked out. We tried two garages that were closed, one that you needed a membership to get a service (it also looked hugely expensive, Dominique felt very out of place), they pointed us in the direction of a garage that you did not need said membership.

"See Ya Later Shit Lords!"

We found the mechanic that spoke English, and he reckoned it would be €40 for the belt itself, which would have to be ordered, and then another €100 for the labour costs. This was something that we could not afford, and it was extortionately overpriced, as the same belt on eBay was £3.49. So we decided to head to a Daewoo/Chevrolet auto parts store just outside Budapest and pass on the trip to Croatia. It would have added a sizeable distance onto our journey, and we wanted Dominique to actually make it out of Europe.

We are currently in Slovenia about 2 hours away. We have booked a hostel for tonight, which is 30 meters from the bar where the pit stop is being held. We are well placed. I will let you know tomorrow, if we get the right parts we need.

"See Ya Later Shit Lords!"

Chapter 9: Hungarian Hunk

21 Jul 2016

I believe we were just on our way to Budapest in the last blog. We were heading to an auto parts shop to get a power steering belt for Dominique. She was getting twitchy as we pulled up in front of a much younger, a more in shape, Hungarian Matiz model. I think if she wasn't red we would have seen Dominique blushing at how tired she was looking. That would soon be fixed with a new belt to accessorise her look (it's all about the confidence) and to mainly make the power steering work again. (I feel as if I have personified the car too much here, I will stop).

Anyway with the belt picked up and ready to be fitted later, we headed into the capital of Hungary. We had booked a hostel the night before, knowing it was close to the bar where the rally pit stop was due to be taking place. It turned out the room was a lot closer than we had first thought. It was literally on a balcony above the bar. You could practically see how cheap the beer was from your bed. I had a feeling we weren't going to be getting the comfortable night's sleep we were hoping. With a name like 'Infinite Party Hostel' I don't really know what we were expecting. The name is suggesting that there is always a party there. There is never not a party happening.[4] The vibe

---

[4] The year is 2051, World War 3 has just ended in all out nuclear warfare. The inevitable has happened, President Trump has nuked Russia. Russia has nuked America. Everyone else has decided to launch their own nuclear missiles, as everyone is inevitably fucked. The human race is on the brink of extinction, just a few hundred people are left on earth. There are food and water shortages throughout the globe, and things are looking very bleak.

Humans look to be going the same way as every other living thing on the planet. All seems lost as there is no hope. In the midst of this nuclear holocaust this small hostel in the back streets of Budapest is still suggesting, by the nature of its name, that there will be a party. I DON'T THINK SO. (I think you get the idea, the party never stopped).

"See Ya Later Shit Lords!"

of the place definitely followed this trend. Then again you can't really complain for £6 a night.

We left the hostel to go and have a look at the sights Budapest has to offer and to get something to eat. We were not disappointed. The walk down to the river, was littered with huge cathedrals and Eastern European buildings. Eight hours down the road from Austria, leads us to this amazing, historically drenched, city, a stark contrast from the mountains, rivers and woodland we had experienced the night before. But that is what I love about the trip. One day is never the same as the previous (apart from the anonymous autobahn). When we reached the river we walked along to the 'Shoes on the Danube', a memorial to those who died in the Second World War.[5] Mikey got into full photographer mode, by lying on the floor, to get the best angle.

We headed back in the direction of the never ending party that was our hostel, looking for somewhere to eat. We stumbled upon a traditional Hungarian restaurant, and we tucked into some goulash.

Back at the hostel, we spruced ourselves up with our first shower (not wash), since we had left Devon. As you would expect from its name, the facilities were not the greatest, they are obviously too busy partying to make sure the shower doors and the curtains actually close. We headed downstairs to join in the festivities. We met two ralliers from Cornwall. We had actually seen them before when they had tried to check into the same hostel as us, only to be told they had

---

[5] The memorial was conceived by a film director Can Togay. It is on the East bank of the Danube River and honours the Jews who were killed by fascist Arrow Cross militiamen in Budapest during WWII. The militiamen ordered the Jews to remove their shoes, before they were then shot at the water's edge. Allowing their bodies to fall into the river and be swept away.

The Arrow Cross Party was a national socialist party, which led a government in Hungary from 15 October 1944 to 28 March 1945. During their short rule ten to fifteen thousand civilians were murdered, mainly Jews and Romanians. A further 80,000 were sent to concentration camps in Austria. The leaders of the party were tried as war criminals after the war was over.

booked their room for a day later. A lucky escape some would say. I also met up with the kind rallier who had picked up my wash bag. My washing items and I were reunited again. We proceeded to meet many more teams, swapping stories of how we had made it to Budapest. Reoccurring questions were asked. "What route are you doing? Oh the southern route. Are you getting the ferry? Oh you are going through Iran, we are getting the ferry to Turkmenistan." It has to be done though, we are looking for friends to convoy with, through the countries where you a most likely to break down.

We awoke early to the sound of silence, the party had finished something I didn't think was possible. Although, according to Mikey, it hadn't finished that much earlier from when I had woken up. I had slept through most of the noise, but I think Mikey was longing for his Love Hammock from the Austrian woods. We wanted to get on the road early, as we wanted to make it to Sofia, the capital of Bulgaria, and then head up to the Rila National Park. There are seven lakes cascading down the mountainside, and it is something I have wanted to see since we signed up for the rally.

We are now blasting down the Serbian motorway, having had our first proper border crossing (we had to show our passports and everything). Mikey pointed out that it was crazy how far you could get in Europe without having to show any form of documentation. Our plan is to find a camping spot near the top of these lakes. Let's hope the Bulgarian park rangers are as friendly as the Belgian ones. Find out how we get on in the next blog.

"See Ya Later Shit Lords!"
Chapter 10: Rila Lake Regret

22 Jul 2016

I shouldn't have mocked the ease of our first border crossing. Everything was going smoothly and we were due to reach the Rila national park by just gone 2100. Giving us time to find a place to set up our hammocks. However the Serbian/Bulgarian border had other ideas. We were stuck in a queue. Nothing seemed to move until one person started honking their horns. This then prompted everyone else to join to in, fed by frustration. I thought this would be a waste of time, but it actually seemed to work. Cars started moving, and when they stopped again for a prolonged period of time, the horns started up again. Naturally, we joined the chorus of car horns, to get the queue moving again. This charade of stop/start lasted a good two hours.

Once we had cleared the border and paid for our Bulgarian vignette (some bullshit sticker/tax for the road, which we have found out, from another team that you do actually need to buy, as they were fined €120 as opposed to its cost of €10) and pushed onto the campsite.

We passed Sofia, after sampling the local delicacy of McDonald's, and decided we wouldn't be able to make it all the way to the top, so we pulled into a track at the base of the mountain and settled down for our first car sleep. All the crap that was in the back was pushed to the boot of the car so the seats could be fully reclined to provide some sort of a make shift bed. A bed that could only be used whilst laying awkwardly flat on your back, any thought of trying to change position throughout the night was out of the question. The stiff back was already upon us.

We woke up early, partly because we wanted to get up to the lakes and back in a reasonable time so we could set off for Romania, but mainly because the light was hitting our eyes from all angles (Mikey's sister was right, eye masks were in order, but they could not be found in our sleepy state the night before). The car was also

"See Ya Later Shit Lords!"

surrounded by wild horses, sniffing around, trying to get a feel of what this shitty red metal box was doing in their back garden. These were not the wild animals I was expecting to encounter in the woods when we were pondering where we should sleep the previous night. I was more worried about wild bears, which is why I was pushing for the uncomfortable sleep in the car rather than the 'love hammocks'. The 'love hammocks' could have quite easily turned into a lovely, conveniently placed, snack for Yogy and his pals, swinging tauntingly in the Bulgarian breeze.

We set off up the mountain to park the car, and stroll to the lakes. We foolishly turned the car around when we got to a man who was asking for parking money, we thought we knew better and tried to get the car closer without paying. We spotted a dirt track which progressed into a path littered with massive rocks allowing our sump guard to be tested for the first time. Eventually we got to a point where the car could go no further, the decision to walk the rest was sort of made for us.

'A two hour round trip', they said. 'Have breakfast when you get back', they said. 'Only take your camera and minimal amounts of water', they said. (I don't know who I am supposing 'they' are, we hadn't asked anybody about this place, not even the car park attendant and we only had ourselves to blame). It looked as if we were off for a wander around a city. We also decided that it would be wise not to take any money. 'You two are fucking morons', they definitely said.

We couldn't have been more wrong. We were severely under prepared for what was about to come. The two hour round trip hike, turned into a three hour marathon from the car to the top of the mountain, where you still couldn't actually see the lakes. We discovered there was a chair lift that runs to just below the summit and we had only walked to the top of the chairlift. It still took us another hour and a half to walk to see the lakes. On our return to the chairlift, as there was no way we were walking back down, we realised that we had brought no money with us. The man controlling the lift was not

"See Ya Later Shit Lords!"

even partial to a cigarette bribe. He said that he didn't smoke, and it would be 20 Lev for the pleasure of riding his chair to the bottom.

We retreated to weigh up our options. We could either walk down, which wasn't really an option, or try and sneak on to the chairlift. In the near distance there were some people talking in English. We ran up to them and explained our situation, they turned out to be a mixture of Americans and Australians. We asked them if we could have 20 Lev so we could get back to our beloved Dominique, she seemed so far away. I transferred the American the equivalent of £8 on PayPal. It's a good job Bulgaria have made sure there is good mobile data at the top of a massive mountain.

The ride on the way down the mountain was fairly peaceful, but we still had to get back to Dominique, which was another 30 minute walk. When we eventually arrived back, we immediately boiled some water to cook some boil in the bags to regain some well needed energy. Six hours after we had set off on our walk everything was packed up and we set off to find our second sight of the day, the Buzludzha, a monument on the way to the Romanian beach party.

No sooner had we set off from our parking spot, I hit one of those fucking huge protruding rocks that I mentioned earlier, it was hidden in the shade and this meant it was time for our first wheel change.[6] We also had to fix the roofbox back into position, as it had been dislodged during the impact. Today was the worst day we had had on the trip so far. Romania seemed a long way off at that moment.

We had learned a valuable lesson that morning, don't just set out naively, underprepared, on an amazing adventure to go and see some idyllic lakes you once read about, actually speak to some local people to get some finer details about the place they are experts on.[7] For

---

[6] This certainly would NOT be our first and only, ladies and gentlemen, don't you worry about that. Stay tuned fans of flat tyres there is plenty more where that came from.

[7] We also forgot we weren't Bear 'Fucking' Grylls.

example, if we had just spoken to that parking attendant he would have told us, 'No, you can't just drive to the top' and suggested how ridiculous it would have been to walk, and he would have invited us to use the perfectly good chairlift.

We reached the Buzludzha, without too many more incidents, in the late afternoon. It looks like Bond villain's HQ, a classic concrete circular building on top of a mountain. It is really eerie, as it is completely empty inside, and you aren't allowed to even go in anymore. I think if we were allowed inside we definitely would have been greeted by a bald man swivelling in a chair stroking a cat. (Something Mikey would have welcomed with open arms). It is situated at the peak of a Balkan mountain and has wild horses roaming around the outside (which scared the shit out of me when I eagerly rounded a corner). It was the place of the last battle between the Bulgarian rebels and the Ottoman Empire. (See, this blog is educational, as well as a laugh a minute). Anyway, we got a few snaps with the car in shot, and then set off for Romania.[8]

This is where I am as I write this, I may have to stop soon as the weaving mountain roads are making feel sick. It was alright when I was driving, and great fun, darting up the mountain, switch-back after switch-back all the way to the top. I hoping we will have a better day tomorrow, filled with less incidents. We are hoping to stay up and see the sunrise over the Black Sea and meet up with our various friends we have already met, if we get there in time.

---

[8] The Buzludzha Monument was built on the peak by the Bulgarian communist regime. It commemorated the events of 1891, when a group of socialists led by Dimitar Blagoev assembled secretly in the area to form an organised socialist movement that led to the founding of the Bulgarian Social Democratic Party, a forerunner of the Bulgarian Communist Party. No longer maintained by the Bulgarian government after 1989 however, it has since fallen into disuse. Currently the monument stands abandoned and vandalised. The roof of the building is heavily damaged, and due to the danger of collapsing metal tiles the main entrance of the building has been closed to the public.

"See Ya Later Shit Lords!"
Chapter 11: Black Sea Sunrise

23 Jul 2016

We arrived at the Romanian Beach Party at around 0230, after what was a mammoth day. Our bodies were willing us to go to sleep, but there was drinking and festivities to be had. Our aim was to stay up and watch the sunrise over the Black Sea.

We got to about two hours to go and decided that we could afford ourselves two hours sleep and set an alarm to see it, therefore headed back to the car to set up our hammocks. However, on our return we bumped into our Irish friends, who had just arrived and looked like they had had a worse day than ours. We couldn't go to bed now, so we swung back by the bar and settled in on sun loungers waiting for the magical time of 0544.

Swapping stories of what had been happening in the past few days was the order of the night. And then there it was, it was so light it also seemed as if it was day time. But we couldn't go to bed until we saw the sun peak it's little head up. When it did, it was definitely worth waiting for. But enough was enough and we headed for our swinging beds.

We were woken by Kieran at around 0800, a mere two hours after we had gone to bed. We had planned to convoy with them today, but their ETD had moved forward considerably from the 1200 agreed time. We said we would meet them in Istanbul to allow us a couple more hours of sleep. We then woke up again, at around 1000, in a pool of sweat and mouth's drier than Gandhi's flip-flop, as there was no protection from the Romanian morning sun. It was time to leave and find some shade.

Sunny Beach was our mid-point destination on our way to Turkey. We wanted a quick refreshing, relaxing, dip in the Black Sea before heading to the border. What we stumbled upon was a much shitter version of Magaluf. (Mikey and I have been to both places and trust me, this was more of a shithole than the one Mikey dug in the Austrian woods). You practically had to queue to get in the sea and when you did actually get in the sea, it was like being crammed into an under-age disco and you basically had to brush past people's shoulder to get to the deep water.

After retrieving our belongings, which had surprising hadn't been stolen, we headed for something to eat. This turned out to be as bad as our swimming experience meaning we quickly set off to fill up our jerry cans at the Bulgarian fuel station, just before the border. This was to try and avoid having to fill up in Turkey at their apparent extortionate prices.

We have just gone through the Bulgarian broader, and are now in the rigmarole of trying to get into Turkey. This involves a lot of exchanging of papers, and money (in their direction) for us to cross under the barrier towards Istanbul. There are a fair few other rally teams here, each one telling the person behind how the system works. It looks like there is some movement so I will leave you for now. Our plan is to head for a hostel we have booked, right under the Haigia Sophia. Fun facts to follow in tomorrow's blog.

"See Ya Later Shit Lords!"
Chapter 12: Birthday Bonanza

24 Jul 2016

We got back on the road again, after our border experience, heading towards Istanbul. There was three hours to go before we hit this famously amazing city. I was in the hot seat, and felt apprehensive and nervous about being in a country that had seen so much unrest, worryingly recently, and we were heading to the eye of the storm.[9]

This feeling was still there but had subsided considerably after we had been going for two hours, we stopped at a toll road. Mikey went to find out what the deal was with the road, as there were no obviously toll collectors. I was left in the car, and was offered some freshly picked pears by a group of lorry drivers who had also congregated at the toll booths. They pointed us in the right direction to pay someone. I thought they would be nice, juicy and ripe because they had been freshly picked. They were mushy and not ripe at all. This was the first act of hospitality that we experienced in this country, and certainly not the last.

I was getting tired with an hour to go, Mikey swapped into the driver's seat for the last bit of driving. As we neared the centre of the city, and our hostel, the volume of traffic increased as the lack of personal space around the car decreased. It was an incredible sight. We turned off and went over a motorway flyover and looked down

---

[9] This has to be made clear at this point. This was a week after the coup that had taken place in cities across Turkey. It was in fact a coup d'état attempt against state institutions, including the government and President Erdogan. The attempt was carried out by a faction within the Turkish Armed Forces. Istanbul and the capital Ankara were the main key places where control was attempted to be seized. However, they failed to do so after forces loyal to the state defeated them. This created a huge stir in these two major cities and shocked the whole world. Mikey and I were watching the events unfold before we left on the rally. This made Turkey one of the main countries we were nervous about traversing.

onto a sea of red, from the rear lights, as the ten lanes of traffic were all trying to merge down to three lanes. It was an incredible sight.

Mikey was loving the city driving, he said described it as like it was a video game. Get to the hostel without bashing any locals. Minus 10 points for pedestrians. This was difficult as there were so many people about, as part of a protest which we believe was in favour of the government after the recent coup. Almost every car was flying their national flag from the windows, as well as being trapped across their bonnet. People were out in droves on the bridges above us. It was like nothing I have seen before, Mikey was in his element.[10]

We eventually arrived at our hostel at around just before midnight. All I wanted was something to eat and to get into bed. We went to the restaurant across the street from our hostel, who offered us some free shisha because of where we were staying. We sat down next to some fellow ralliers, Henry and Rob (or Frosty), who were engineers in the Royal Navy (which later transpired to be the RFA, which isn't the real Navy) they said to try the food. And the beer. And the shisha. They weren't wrong. All three were exquisite. My mood was perking up, these guys were so friendly and we were getting on like a house on fire. Mikey was struggling to keep up with the navy and engineering lingo, I had to translate some of the acronyms. As I was in a better mood, Mikey reminded me that it was technically my birthday, I was having such a great time I had failed to remember that I had turned 22 a good two hours ago.

One beer turned into many, and one flavour of shisha turned into us having four on the go at once. We had a new game, blow the biggest shisha bubble and try to get it to float off into the night sky. When this was achieved it was followed an increasingly slurred 'See you later, Shit lord' by Frosty in his northern accent. Who had also gone to the toilet and had mistaken the well-known face of Tom Cruise (who was obviously chosen to adorn the men's door for this

---

[10] I have seen something similar in terms of volume of traffic in India. But this was the first time I had been part of a mass protest on this scale.

"See Ya Later Shit Lords!"

very reason), for John Barrowman. He was convinced the Barrowman was a huge hit in Turkey.

We were once again swapping stories of what had been happening on the rally so far. It turned out they are on a similar route to ours and they are finishing early like us. So hopefully we will meet them again at the ferry. The story swapping carried on until about 0300 when another rally team, of Americans, turned up. They had driven down from the same place as us, in Romania, but had had two and half hour wait at the border. They were keen for beers, so it kept flowing. More outstanding hospitality was in order, by the waiters of the restaurant, as they kept the place open until we had left.

Eventually the Americans retired to bed, but the party for the originals kept going until 0600.[11] where we decided to go and look at the Haigi Sofia,[12] as there would be no crowds. It was absolutely stunning, and like no other building I had seen before. The city is famous for where Christianity and Islam clash, and this building was the epicentre, as it is both a church and a mosque. It was awe inspiring.

We left Henry and Frosty at their hostel, and were nearly in our beds, when we saw a van with Mongol rally stickers on it from last year. The guy sat next to it preceded to try and sell us the van that had three flat tyres. He then went on to tell us his life story and pose for pictures. We just wanted to get to bed. Eventually we made it there.

We awoke at 0955 this was the latest we could get up, as check out was at 1000, and wanted to go and visit some more of the sights Istanbul had to offer. We set off with the mother of all hangovers, it wasn't like we had to drive 8 hours to Cappadocia or anything (Oh wait!). Again Istanbul surprised us with its fantastic sights. On our return to the hostel, and Dominique, we were approached by a man

---

[11] A feat that I'm sure Gerrard and his Liverpool team mates would not be strangers, after that fateful night back in '05.

[12] Hagia Sophia was a Greek orthodox chrisitian church, it later became an imperial mosque and is now a museum.

who owned a rug shop. He said for us to come in and have a look. Mikey and I both went into the shop for 'Just a look' with no intention of buying a rug. I don't know how this happened, but we both left his shop with two rugs for 300 lira (£60), half an hour later. He had bamboozled us into buying these rugs. He assured us that the rugs were worth 10 times what we had paid. So we were happy with our deal. Why would he lie?

Having crossed over the Bosphorus river, into Asia, we are now on our way to Cappadocia, where we hope to stay in some caves and go hot air ballooning tomorrow. I think of the pears as the classic 'Don't judge a book by its cover', very fitting for our time in Istanbul. Even though their country and city is in turmoil, the people were some of the most hospitable folk I have ever met. For a place that we were just going to blast through, scared, I am so glad we didn't. Istanbul you have been amazing.

"See Ya Later Shit Lords!"
Chapter 13: Getting Air in Asia

25 Jul 2016

The drive down from Istanbul to Cappadocia was fairly uneventful, other than the suspicious meat we ate for lunch in a Turkish service station. We thought it might have an effect on us later, but we seem to have ridden out the worst of it. Our British stomachs were tested and they passed. Bring on the Mongolian yak testicles.

We arrived at our cave hostel at around 2230, the place was amazing. Much nicer than the two hostels we had experienced before, and there wasn't a continuous party in sight. We were ready for a good night's sleep. But not before we had asked the hostel guy what time the hot air balloon tours started in the morning. He lets us know that we would have to be ready for 0400. We weren't going to get as much sleep as we had first thought. But he did say we would get two breakfasts, one with the tour company and one back at the hostel. This made the whole getting up early bearable.

0400 came along far too early and we boarded the minibus still half asleep. We were driven to another hotel, where the first 'breakfast' was served. I was expecting a huge platter to arrive and a buffet style traditional Turkish breakfast to ensue. Instead the Turks believe to think that a roll and a water is sufficient as 'breakfast'. I wasn't too chuffed about this. Still the one back at our hostel was bound to pull it out of the bag.

After the poor excuse for breakfast, we were taken to the launch site where there were around six balloons being fired up. The hour long experience was absolutely incredible. We rose up to around 600m, with more and more balloons appearing from different launch sites. We spiralled over the famous sandstone caves of Cappadocia, dipping in and out of the craggy outcrops. It was a magical feeling being so peaceful, until the pilot blasted more hot air into the canvas above our heads to keep us afloat. As the balloon drifted up and down, the sun started to rise over mountains. We have seen some amazing sunsets and sunrises so far on the trip and this one was up

"See Ya Later Shit Lords!"

there (literally). The best thing is that I know there are a lot more in store, especially when we get to the deserts.

The pilot guided us to the landing point, skilfully parking us on the back of a trailer. We jumped out and were treated with non-alcoholic champagne and a certificate to say that we had survived. It must be pretty awkward for the guy who had already written all the names on the certificates, if the balloon doesn't make it back to the landing area safely. I imagine he would just have to watch, certificates and champagne substitute in hand, as the balloon drifted off over the mountains. I would like to think he would shout, in the style of Frosty, 'See ya later, shitlords', as if we were the bubbles back in Istanbul.

Anyway this was not the case and we were dropped off back at our hostel, and went back to much needed sleep, with the thought that we would wake up at 0900 to give our washing to a laundry company, which was long overdue. But we were both so tired that we slept through our alarms, and woke up just before our second 'breakfast' was served, having missed the laundry by a long way. (It would have to wait until Azerbaijan). This hostel had done one better, by providing two hard boiled eggs each. Come on Turkey, you need to step up your breakfast game.

Retiring to our rooms allowed us to get all our stuff in order, and to use the WiFi to update our previous blogs and Facebook pages. We are now on our way to Samsun in northern Turkey, on the coast of the Black Sea. It is a relatively short five hour drive, compared to the eight or nine hours we have been used to during the past few days. We are in need of a lie in, hopefully the hammocks will provide this tonight, as we are looking for somewhere to camp.

"See Ya Later Shit Lords!"
Chapter 14: Kebabs and Tyres

26 Jul 2016

I take it back about the Turkish and their food portions. They may not know how to do breakfast, but my word they know how sort out a lunch. We were about 3 hours outside of Samsun and had decided to stop at a road side restaurant for lunch. This was no Little Chef equivalent, it was an upmarket establishment, which looked out of place on the side of the road. We pulled up and went in for a light snack, before getting back to the driving.

The language barrier was apparent from the beginning but before we had even tried to order something, there were dishes already upon us. Four of them, accompanied by dinner plate sized flat breads. We thought this would be a nice starter to the kebabs we actually wanted for a main. Again, before we could point out the kebabs we desired, more dishes arrived, potatoes and onions. We eventually got the waiters attention and pointed at 'doner kebab'. We thought that was the end of it. However the waiter came back over and pointed to 'shish kebab' as if to say there were no more doner left. So we said we would take it.

Before we knew it, the doner was delivered swiftly followed by a mountain of shish kebabs, the waiter promised us that there was no more on the way. We had ourselves a man vs food eating challenge on our hands. Everything was so delicious but there was no way we could finish it all. The waiter came back once no more food could be consumed (not something I take lightly), and asked if we wanted 'tea'. We said 'of course', when in Rome and all that. Five minutes later a Turkish coffee arrived, not tea. This was probably one of the best meals that we have both had, where we've had no control over what we wanted or what was coming next, all for around £12 each.

Dominique had to carry us, and the extra food weight, up to Samsun in the north of Turkey. We had planned to meet up with Henry and Frosty at the Municipality Campsite which was located right on the coast but still close enough to the city to taste the traffic.

"See Ya Later Shit Lords!"

It wasn't the idyllic Turkish campsite you had in mind, trust me. For £3 a night and it had perfectly spaced poles to hang our hammocks, it wasn't all that bad.

We met four Italian teams, who had started in the north of Italy rather than Goodwood, and also another English team. All were sharing the campsite with us. Whilst the Italians made their pasta dinner (That's not a racist/stereotypical slur because it actually happened, wasn't a cheap joke), we chatted to Elliot, Lauren, and Ferghal (The Brits). It turned out that they all worked in TV/acting, and it also seemed as if they were the rally gossips. They were sharing stories about their jobs and other people they had met on the rally, both of which interested both Mikey and me greatly. It was a shame that we would probably not cross paths we these guys again, as they were headed to Iran and had a longer timescale to ours. We retired to our hammocks to get a sensible night's sleep for the drive to Batumi. The sound of the traffic on the motorway overpass above us and the street lights were almost as much of a calming influence as the river in Austria.

We awoke relatively and unsurprisingly early, giving us enough time to go and have breakfast with Henry and Frosty, who had decided to stay in a hostel rather than the campsite. We tried driving to said hostel, but it was a maze of back streets and one way systems, so we decided to meet them in Batumi instead. On the way out of the city we came across a tyre shop and thought it would be a good opportunity to fix THAT tyre from the Rila lakes regret.

What would have normally been a ten minute job, if the mechanic and us both spoke the same language, became a two and a half hour saga. The language barrier was again clear from the beginning. Many wheel rims and tyres were shown and tested, similar to the 'Rug Tinder' we had played a couple of days previously in Istanbul, before he found one that fitted. Then he spotted that another of our rims was rusty and gestured that it should be changed. So after another half an hour of trying to understand what we both meant, it was changed as well. We then thought it would be a good idea to get another spare wheel, for the desert driving, while we were here. That took yet more time to explain.

We eventually had two new rims and three new tyres, and we settled on a price of 250 lira, which seemed fairly reasonable to us, if not slightly over priced. This was until we got about a mile down the road, where there was an almighty vibration in the steering wheel when exceeding 50mph. I stuck my head out the window and I could see the wheel was not attached properly and I was shocked that it was still actually clinging on at all. I pulled over and we swapped back to our original rims and head back to the tyre shop. He had obviously thought he had got rid of those crazy foreigners, but we got out both wheels and showed him that they didn't fit properly. He agreed and set about grinding away the metal that was interfering. I had thought originally when the wheel was fitted, that it didn't look right, by I trusted his expertise. For someone whose daily profession this is, the whole affair was shoddy at best. Surely knowing whether a tyre is fitted properly translates through any language?

Anyway with all seven tyres now fitting properly we are on our way to Batumi, which is the first major city on the Georgian side of the Turkey/Georgia border. We are about three hours away, with four wheels still attached, on the coast road. There is the Black Sea to the left of us and mountains on our right, another beautiful region that Turkey has to offer. That three hours left could be extended, as we have heard stories that we are probably in for a long wait at the border. I'll update you tomorrow.

Chapter 15: Border Boredom

27 Jul 2016

    The border crossing between Turkey and Georgia was our easiest so far, it was only a mere 8 HOUR WAIT! We arrived at the border through a tunnel which spat us out at the front of the queue, at around 2000. We were quickly told to join the back of the queue by a smug looking border guard. We thought it couldn't be that long, but as we kept driving past the locals and other rally teams, who had said they had already been there 4 hours, we started to think we were going to be in for the long haul.

    We were indeed. The time was filled with a mixture of films, sleep, and walking to and from the shop. We had to take it in turns to sleep, because one person had to be on guard to move the car up in the queue. If whoever was driving fell asleep, angry locals would either honk until you were awake, or the more sneaky ones wouldn't honk and just drive around you and steal your place. Henry and Frosty, who we were going to meet up with in Batumi just the other side of the border, arrived at around 0000 after having had issues with their car. We let them know they were going to in it for the long haul too.

    Turkey was such a great country on this trip and we were sad to be leaving the friendly people and the places it had to offer, but when we eventually rolled into Georgia at 0400 we were so glad to be out of that queue. There was also a one hour time difference we had to contend with, so we had even less time to sleep. We pulled into a layby and settled in for our second car sleep.

    We were awoken two and a half hours later by three Georgians, who were gesturing that this was their layby and that we should move on swiftly, not after taking cigarettes for the privilege of telling us, the cheeky bastards. We thought we might as well push on to Tbilisi, taking it in turns to sleep and drive, as there was nothing really in between.

"See Ya Later Shit Lords!"

The twisting mountain roads made it difficult to sleep, but the jaw dropping views made up for it. It's amazing how you can come just a few miles over the border and the landscape is completely different to the previous place. Every time we rounded a corner another picturesque scene greeted us, rivers, mountains, and winding asphalt that wouldn't look out of place on a Georgian postcard. It was another breath-taking drive.

With the changing scenery came the change of driving style, this had been noticeable in most of the countries we had passed through, but it was more evident now. Even though the Turks cut you up, whenever they overtook, at least they had a bit of common courtesy to let you out once in a while and were quite skilled with it. Whereas the Georgians took no prisoners, they would overtake on a blind bend without hesitation, and a straight bit of road was an absolute free-for-all. You had to adapt your own driving style otherwise you would be caught out, the polite British way doesn't cut it out here.

Another thing we have both noticed is that when there are only a few major cities in a country, driving allows you to see every aspect of the country. For example with Georgia, we started in the most rural part, right near the border, where the cows roamed free and the laws on inbreeding seemed to be relaxed. As we got closer to the city the metropolis seemed to appear out of the mountains, and no doubt when we leave for Azerbaijan, more of the rural will greet us. I suppose it's just how a classic city works, but it is strange to see it happen so rapidly and all in one day.

We have now arrived in Tbilisi, after a long old slog, which was broken up by a swim in one of the beautiful rivers I mentioned earlier. It was a perfect swimming hole that seemed very popular with the locals, who all were staring at us as we rocked up in Dominique. We are staying in a hostel for two nights, allowing us to meet up with a few ralliers, wash our clothes, and gain some rest for the assault on Baku and the famously unreliable ferry to Turkmenistan.

"See Ya Later Shit Lords!"

Chapter 16: Tbilisi Baths

28 Jul 2016

As it was our rest day, very little has happened worth blogging about. So this will be the shortest one by a long way.

We arrived in Tbilisi at around 1600. This gave us time to sort our shit out. Such us repack the car, which is becoming a daily occurrence, (during a drive everything gets moved from its right position when you are trying to grab something from the passenger seat, both of our OCD means that it has to be repacked and everything has to be in its place), wash our clothes and wash ourselves.

Once this was completed, we went out for some food, shisha and beers with Henry and Frosty and some other ralliers who happened to be in Tbilisi at the same time as us. Most were moving on tomorrow towards Baku, one team had been stuck here for two days repairing their car after having a run in with a Mercedes. Again stories were swapped, this is a must when you meet new ralliers. We tried to get into a casino, but apparently flip-flops and shorts are not an appropriate dress code, but somehow Frosty's German pornstar boots and shorts were acceptable. We had to get a taxi back to our hotel, as Mikey and I had no idea how to get back.

Mikey and I both woke up at around the same time, four in the afternoon, we were long overdue a lie in. We had not had a proper night's sleep for a week. We really went to town on the rest day and eventually gathered our thoughts and got up around 1630. It turns out Henry and Frosty, who had been in another hotel the night before, had already had breakfast and lunch, and had checked in to the room opposite ours for another night. We are going to convoy and hopefully get the ferry with them tomorrow.

The rest day continued as we have just got back from a sulphur bath and sauna experience, which was delightful. We are sprucing ourselves up for another evening in Tbilisi. We are going to go up

"See Ya Later Shit Lords!"

the funicular railway to the TV tower, which is on one of the mountains that overlooks the city. After the views, we are then going to head to the casino, with appropriate footwear. I will let you know how the evening goes, in the next blog, as we head to Baku. This is probably one of the most vital parts of the trip, and the part we are most worried about. The ferry is very unreliable and bribes have to exchange hands to actually get your car on the boat. It could screw up the whole timescale of the trip, but we live in hope.

"See Ya Later Shit Lords!"
Chapter 17: Lucky Escape

29 Jul 2016

Last night we relaxed around camp again, went for a relaxing sulphur bath experience, followed by dinner just below the TV tower, on the mountain that overlooks the city. A short funicular railway ride gave us access to some delicious Georgian cuisine and some stunning views of the city (something my shitty phone camera could not do justice). We returned to the strip of bars we had been the night before, and tried to gain access to the allusive casino. It turns out that they not only don't accept flip flops and shorts, they are just not keen on shorts as a whole. That idea was quickly canned and we headed for bed.

0930 was the time we surfaced, we were packed up and ready to go for 1030, after a wheel change. We had a slow puncture that had worked its magic throughout the night, I can safely say we were ripped off by that Turkish tyre man. So annoying. We eventually got on the road towards Azerbaijan in our new convoy with team "Pug Crawlers" (Henry and Frosty), once breakfast was suitably dispatched. This was partly to make sure we had the most important meal of the day on board, but mostly to steal the Wi-Fi so we could navigate out of the city making sure we were heading to Baku not Batumi. (Classic mistake getting your Batumi's mixed up with your Baku's).

It was great being in a convoy at last, and everything was going smoothly until we neared the border. We had been adopting the Georgian style of driving, but not to their same extremes. Basically we were overtaking when we could, on the straights, otherwise we would still be stuck behind a line of Lada's in two weeks' time.

A straight bit of road opened up and the van in front was slowing down, as if to let us overtake, however according to Mikey and the Pug Crawlers, who were behind (as I was looking down at the map at the time), the van put his indicator on and started turning left when we were already pretty much alongside. Mikey slammed on the brakes as soon as he saw the situation going south, leaving some fat eleven's in the road. We ended up clipping our mirror on his, knocking the glass out. This development quickly took my attention away from the navigation and we finally skidded to a halt in a grass ditch about forty metres down the road. Shaken, but both unscathed.[13]

Henry and Frosty pulled in and ran over to see if we were alright, the driver of the van was shouting at us in Georgian, locals gathered around the incident at an alarming rate. We thought the situation was going even more Pete Tong. However, eventually, one of the locals waved us on, as everything seemed to be alright with the driver. There was no real damage on either of the cars, if anything we had improved his shitty van (given it character). We set off and quickly realised the incident had given us our second puncture of the day. Leaving us with just one good spare tyre, the same amount as before the Turkish mechanic had his way with us.

The mood became sombre in the car, as the shock and adrenaline wore off, we were both reflecting on how lucky we had just been and how different things could have played out. It's one of those things where you never fully remember what happened thirty minutes after the incident, because everything happened so quickly and was fuelled with adrenaline. But it's definitely something you don't forget.

We are all alright now, we have just come through the Azerbaijan/Georgia border, which was much less painful than our previous crossing. All the paperwork and car checks were completed within an hour, and we are sitting in the fine country of Azerbaijan waiting for our convoy to reform.

---

[13] I was trying to remember the other day how this had actually happened when the van was turning left. But I forgot that we were driving on the right-hand side of the road, as had been the case since we had left the UK. It probably would have been wise to complete the trip in a left-hand drive car, but we wouldn't have had nearly as much fun riding shotgun for each other.

"See Ya Later Shit Lords!"

We will then head on towards Baku and the ferry. Mikey has been in contact with a guy called Ismail (who seems like the most legit person in the whole country). He has promised to get us on the ferry on Sunday and make sure all our visas are in order, for a small fee of course. First we have a couple of days in the capital. Our first night is in a hostel and the second is in the luxurious Holiday Inn (which I booked without a cancellation clause by accident a good few months before we even set off, but I won't steal Mikey's thunder in this blog). As always, I will let you know how everything pans out.

"See Ya Later Shit Lords!"

Chapter 18: Park Anywhere

30 Jul 2016

After the relatively painless border crossing, we were into the country of Azerbaijan. It is a place that I had not really known too much about. All I knew was that the 'Polis' were meant to pull you over a lot, it had had the F1 fairly recently, and you only had 3 days in the country otherwise you had to pay an immigration fee. Our lack of knowledgequickly changed once Frosty had read the wiki travel page and imparted the knowledge he had just learned. Such facts included, you weren't allowed to wear shorts and smiling was an insult. This, and all the other facts, turned out to be untrue, as Mikey and I waltzed around the town where we stopped for lunch in our shorts whilst smiling and waving at everyone. The locals were loving it.

The roads on the way to Baku were different from Georgia, just as shit, but the potholes were replaced by undulating Tarmac. This reduced progress, more so than the potholes, as Dominique was bouncing around all over the shop. This meant we couldn't drive above 60mph. It took a fair while to reach some decent roads to make actual progress, but we were in a convoy and nothing could stop us.

We eventually reached the promise-land of flat roads and pushed on towards our destination, the capital on the Caspian. The motorway driving was broken up by another awesome stretch over the mountains. I was at the helm, loving the hairpin turns (obviously taking more precautions after our previous incident that day). The roads, unfortunately for the fun of driving but good for progress, turned back into motorway and we powered onwards. We stopped on a gravel verge just after some roadworks to go for a piss and I let Mikey into the hot seat. (This has now meant Dominique is filled up with stones in random places and she keeps shitting out random bits of gravel as we drive around Baku).

We eventually made it to the hostel in Baku at about 0100. It is an unbelievable city, in stark contrast to the rest of the country we have driven through, even more so than Georgia. I haven't been to

"See Ya Later Shit Lords!"

Dubai, but I can feel the similarities it shares from people that have. Anyway we arrived at the hostel, after two drunk locals 'helped' us park the cars (I think the shouting and gesturing hindered more than helped). We followed precariously positioned signs that eventually guided us up to the hostel through backstreets and found the owner. She showed us in, through a door that led straight into a ten bed dormitory. It was a very odd experience. People were in their beds, no one was asleep. They were on their phones. Lights went on and off. Face-timing was apparently kosher at 0200. It was a bizarre experience.

We woke up in the morning, and decided to get to our accidental Holiday Inn, as soon as possible. We jumped in the wagons and rolled down the Baku F1 starting grid, to our Holiday Inn. We couldn't actually check in until 1400 but as long as we were away from that sweaty bunk bed sardine tin, we were happy. We asked if we could park our cars in the underground car park. We were met by the head of security and he said this would be no problem. The barrier lifted and we rolled down the ramp. Underground, the security man asked us how long we were staying. We replied that we were staying for one night. He said 'No Problem, park anyway'. Mikey pulled into the nearest space. He came up to the window and said 'can you please park over there instead' gesturing at another space further down the car park. Mikey obliged, pulling the car into said space. The security guard gestured with his hands that he wasn't happy with the position of the car. The car was moved closer to the one next to us. This wasn't right either. Eventually he pointed at the car that was facing out of the space. Mikey turned the car around. It had gone from 'Park the car anywhere' to 'park the car in this specific spot, with this specific orientation'. It wasn't the end of the world, but I found it quite hilarious.

The time before the check in also gave us time to meet Ismail. We met him outside KFC and he said he would sort out the ferry for the cars and us, for a reasonable coordination fee of $30 on top of the $460 ferry fee. Ismail had now become Legismail (Legit Ismail). All we had to do was meet up with him later on in the day, hand over

"See Ya Later Shit Lords!"

our coordination fee, Passports, and documents and we would be put on the next available ferry. We are assured this is going to be tomorrow afternoon. But we will see. I still remain sceptical, even though he warned us not to be.

The remainder of the day was filled with relaxing activities. Pool and spa at the holiday inn, and then food, beer, and shisha out in the town. You might be thinking that this Mongol rally, isn't all that hard. Ed and Mikey seem to be getting pissed and living the highlife every day. I promise you this will be the last hotel/hostel we stay in, until we get to Ulan Bataar/Ulan Ude. There is a long three weeks of camping in the desert ahead of us, trying to stop camel spiders eating our faces. So we are not feeling too guilty about our lifestyle at the moment.

I will write a blog tomorrow, hopefully on the ferry, about how everything got sorted and how everything was fine. It may not be posted for a while. As you probably guessed, desert camping doesn't have the best of Wi-Fi facilities. But I will post when I can. You may get a five edition blog dump all in one when we do eventually use the Turkmenistan Dial-up. Lucky you.

"See Ya Later Shit Lords!"
Chapter 19: Still in Baku

31 Jul 2016

We still haven't managed to get on the ferry, this blog may be even shorter than the one I said would be the shortest of the lot. We waited around all day today. Changing locations, but still making sure we had Wi-Fi. We were waiting for the magic text from Ismail to let us know whether there was going to be a ferry or not. (Title might have given it away).

We started off in the bar of the Holiday Inn, overstaying our check out time by a long way. We eventually got bored of this and moved for a change in scenery. We went to pick up our laundry and to get some dollars out to pay for the ferry, when it eventually arrived. This involved many taxis, who did not have a clue where they were going and charged us extra for the privilege of getting lost with them.

After all the jobs were done we went to a coffee shop in a swanky mall, making sure we had Wi-Fi, to kill some more time. There was still a fair amount of time to wait before Ismail was due to let us know. We then had to have a change of scenery from our change of scenery. So we went back to the Holiday Inn to sponge even more facilities off them by blagging our way into the pool and spa, using our previous room numbers, this killed a lot of time. By the time we had finished in the pool, the fateful text had arrived. "No Ferry Today".

Although this was frustrating, as this was trip was about driving and not the waiting for a ferry, there was literally nothing we could do about it. Having said that we knew this was always going to be the hardest part to negotiate and it is "What the rally is about", which now seems to be a continuing mantra of the trip.

We are certain Ismail is legit and is not trying to screw us over, so we have to trust him. We are also still on track if we get the ferry tomorrow, but that extra day would have been nice seeing as we are on quite a tight schedule. All we could do was try and find somewhere for the night.

We tried playing the charity rally card for a discounted room at the Holiday Inn but this returned with a 'Computer says No' situation. A hotel in the centre of town was booked only to find out there was just one room instead of two, finally we rang Ismail again and he sorted us out a triple room with an extra bed. For a reasonable price of course. We are now just about to head out for food and praying to the ferry gods for the arrival of a boat into Baku tomorrow.

"See Ya Later Shit Lords!"

Chapter 20: Still No Sign of Ferry

01 Aug 2016

So I keep say these blogs are the shortest they will ever be, but the more time we spend in Baku the less there is to say really. We were told by Ismail to meet him at a monument, just by the Holiday Inn.

We thought this was it, we thought his was the day we had been waiting for. There were nine teams, Ismail arrived and gestured for us to follow him. We were the first behind him with the pug crawlers behind us. It was a struggle to keep up with Ismail on the busy road, but there was no option we had to keep up with him and weaving in and out of the traffic across six lanes was the only way we knew how.

We arrived at the ferry entrance which turned out to be literally around the corner. From there I went and registered our passports and car for the 'ferry'. We drove through the barrier and we were told to park up in the holding pen. We thought the ferry was due at any moment. However Ismail told us to leave and await a text from him. He was asked one too many times, by Frosty, if there was going to be a ferry, and he said 'it is like trying to find a black cat in a dark room, I do not know when there will be a ferry.' Mikey remained in his good books though.

We went to Starbucks and McDonald's to make sure we had Wi-Fi to receive the fateful text from Ismail, again. We eventually got bored of Ronald's establishment and headed to a local Hamam Turkish baths. (It still had Wi-Fi). This place was amazing. It had random paintings, statues, and busts of dictators, actresses, and general famous faces covering the walls and interior from all different eras.[14] We paid 19 manat for unlimited use of the sauna, steam rooms, and Turkish baths. We also were treated to a VIP room for no extra cost,

---

[14] Yes, there was an oil painting of Joseph Stalin riding a bear. Why did you even ask? Of course there was, silly question.

which had complimentary food. It was an extra 20 manat for a massage, which we all indulged.

The custom was to go naked, with just a towel around you. When the towel got wet another dry one was waiting for you. The swimming trunks were not needed in Turkish baths. We relaxed and drank beers for a good six hours. This Mongol Rally isn't too hard. With still no news from Ismail, Mikey texted him, indirectly asking if the ferry was leaving, saying 'should we book a hotel for this evening?' He replied yes, which meant there was no ferry today either. We went for some food, and then checked in to our precautionary booked hotel, which we were able to cancel if the ferry did leave, and settled down for another night in Baku. We hope the ferry will leave tomorrow. Otherwise it may start compromising the rest of the trip, which would be a great shame.

"See Ya Later Shit Lords!"
Chapter 21: Hotel Chuck-a-left

02 Aug 2016

Yesterday was another day full of empty promises. We arrived at the port, after an urgent text from Ismail saying that we needed to be down to buy our tickets as soon as possible. We raced out of the hotel as quickly as we could, we didn't even have time for our daily swim and sauna that had become a regular occurrence. We arrived at the port for around 1200 ish. (I can't actually remember because the days have just blurred into one). We were told that there were three boats ready to leave today, one at 1400, one at 1700, and one at 2000, and that we would definitely be leaving today. This was great news and things were looking up. (We knew about as much as Jon Snow about what was to come)[15].

There was lots of procrastinating in the sun, going to the mall for food, trying to play football but being told, in no uncertain terms, that 'no fun was allowed', by the guards. It was ridiculous. That co-ordination fee we had paid Ismail had seemed to have gone to absolute shit, he had no real influence at all. He became the guy that handed the passports to Victoria, the woman who actually had the authority to issue tickets. When he did try and assert some sort of power, the Rally teams that had not gone through Ismail, understandably kicked off. Rifts were starting to show between not just Ismail and teams, but between the Mongol Rally teams. This whole ferry debacle seemed to break the bond we automatically shared by undertaking this challenge. The spirit of the rally was being tested. There had to be some sort of order, Ismail or no Ismail, we had still been here for a good five days now, that must mean something.

It took from when we arrived to around 2200 to actually obtain a ticket to the ferry, we were one of the last teams to actually get our

---

[15] For those that don't frequent Game of Thrones, that means 'The square root of fuck all'.

"See Ya Later Shit Lords!"

tickets through Ismail, I think Mikey was beginning to slip as Ismail's favourite. However, we now have the tickets in our grubby little mits and it is more precious than most of the possessions in the car. (Even the kettle that supplies Mikey with coffee to fuel him for the driving). Those three ferries that were promised obviously turned out to be bullshit. Having got the ticket meant you could buy access on to the ferry, by paying for the 'bridge'. Another stupid way of getting even more money out of us.

With the very sweaty day out of the way, we headed for food, Wi-Fi, and yet another night in a hotel. The food was much more traditional than the pizza and burgers we had had the previous nights. We were ready for the hotel again, and we hailed yet another taxi. Mikey was directing the driver to the hotel, using the GPS on his phone. The driver was getting off track, just like every other taxi experience in Baku. No taxi driver seems to know where anything is in the city, so Mikey told him to 'Chuck a left' (as in to turn left) to get back on the road to the hotel. The driver thought 'Chuck a left' was the name of the hotel, and shouted out the window to a nearby Polis car 'something, undistinguishable words in Azeri, "Hotel Chuck-a-left?"' The polis man had no idea what the driver was on about, so he said it again. Meanwhile, we were all in the back of the taxi giggling like little girls. It had really brightened up a day that had been wholly shit.

The hotel was much worse than the few we had been staying in previously, the quality of the hotels have seemed to diminish the longer we stay in this limbo. Anyway it is a bed, and we can only hope that tomorrow brings us more luck.

Chapter 22: See Ya Later Shit Lords

03 Aug 2016

WE HAVE FINALLY FUCKING LEFT BAKU! I am writing this in my bunk, having just seen us drop all lines from Azerbaijan. I am sleeping in sheets that your grandma wouldn't furnish her house with; it is swelteringly hot; and the ferry ride could take just as long as the wait to embark. But I don't care. We have finally left the place we have been trapped for nearly six days.

Let me take you back to how we started this morning. We were told yesterday to arrive at the port for around 1100, as there would be a ferry leaving at 1400. We now knew that you could add three hours onto anything you were quoted, but we weren't taking our chances, there was no way we were missing this ferry. We arrived at around 1030. We got to our car and after a short wait we were told to move our car to an intermediate holding area just 100 metres closer to a ferry we still could not see. It was progress.

We saw Ismail, he said not to leave this area as we were due to board in 15 minutes. Three hours later we were still in the same spot. There were so many rumours floating around the camp, no one really knew what was going on. Ismail was once again turning into the guy that had no say in anything to do with the port, after saying earlier that morning that he was the King of the Port. We were starting to think our $30 was going towards nothing other than his back pocket, but it had got us this far and ahead of teams who were still in the 'Jungle'. Henry made a valid comparison to how our situation was a snapshot of the Calais 'Jungle'. Our experience is to travel around a third of the world, however we will go back to our 'privileged' lifestyles once this adventure has finished. Whereas the refugee's and migrant's 'adventure' is their life. We have obviously never experienced a fraction of the helplessness and suffering they have, but being in such a situation really does give you a better perspective of what is must be like and why they need the help. You are at the mercy of the authorities who feed you snippets of information, whether it is

"See Ya Later Shit Lords!"

truth or lie, but you have to cling on to something to give you hope to get through the state of limbo. It has been a massive eye opener to something I had not previously considered.

Obviously there was no ferry at 1400, surprise surprise Ismail was bullshitting, but we were told one was unloading and that we would be on the reload. At lot more waiting around, reading, chatting, and general procrastination happened until around 1700. We had the name of the ferry we were on, but no one knew whether we could go. One team, followed closely by another, tested the waters when the guard was not at his post. We were all in our cars, revving our engines, waiting to see if they would be stopped. The rotund guard eventually flagged them down and radioed to see if this was kosher. It was. I put my foot flat to the floor. It was the most action Dominique had seen in a few days, but she responded like a dream. It felt like we were at Goodwood again, back to the place where no rules applied. Frosty and Henry had somehow managed to weave to the front, Mikey and I made it to the back of the two water testers. We were flooring it round to the ferry. It was like a scene out of a minimal budget Need for Speed. We saw the ramp to board the ferry. We had all completely forgotten that we actually needed to go through passport control to leave Azerbaijan. This only crossed our minds once the Pug Crawlers were waved angrily back down the ramp. Mikey and I somehow made it to the front of the reformed queue, once the border guard had organised the chaos. We all just wanted to leave, badly.

Every one, of the lucky ten team boarding party, was processed within the hour. However we had to wait for the unbelievable number of Lorries to be loaded, the real money makers and reason for this ship to go to Turkmenbashi in the first place, we were just after thoughts. We were told it would be another hour until we boarded. Obviously three hours was added on to that, so the time was filled with football and music. Football was allowed in this fun part of the port, the guards seemed to give less of a shit now we were technically out of the country. The music duties seemed to fall on Team Bataar Late Than Never's shoulders, as we were at the front of the queue.

"See Ya Later Shit Lords!"

We dutifully obliged by taking requests and fading in and out of songs, which was the limit of my DJ skills. I like to think we didn't disappoint.

Eventually we were summoned to board, at around 2200, we hadn't been forgotten about. All ten cars were safely on board and we were shown to the room that served 'foodstuff' (the timetable for meals was labelled 'Foodstuff Times') and then to our cabins. They were still loading more Lorries in to the spaces below, so that took another two hours. We played poker with two French guys in the meantime, using cocktail sticks as chips. We finished just as the ferry pushed away from Baku, at 0015. The time is important as Mikey and I have a bet on how long the ferry will take - my guess is 18 hours 37mins, Mikey's 19 hours. I think that is us up to date, this probably won't surface for a good few days due to the lack of Wi-Fi. As I said, you will be lucky enough to have a few to read at once.

"See Ya Later Shit Lords!"
Chapter 23: Turkmenistan Torment

04 Aug 2016

The cabin remained as hot as I described in the last blog, it was absolutely stifling. I had to have a 'timeout', at around 0300, just to cool off, but just climbing back into the top bunk induced yet more sweating. Despite this, everyone seemed to manage sleep until around 1130, getting rid of a large chunk of the ferry passage. We were woken to the Ship's 'Dinner Lady' calling us for Foodstuff, of the lunch variety. I think it is called foodstuff because not even they know what they were serving. There was noodles, cucumber, tomato, and a mystery meat all served with a soup based undertone. It was different to say the least. And not very filling. Or very tasty. The food seemed to pass through me easier than most, and I had to use the stand-up toilet twice more than one would have liked. It was no 'Brown lake and log' situation from Brussels, but it was still pretty bad.

Yet more time passing was undertaken on the ferry, this included: sleeping, trivia games, reading, chatting, blogging, and the card game Slam (which ended at least 5-0 to me against Mikey, I'm writing it here to annoy him when he reads this back). This brought us to the second foodstuff of the day, which was definitely recycled lunch foodstuff. The meat seemed much more mysterious. After the delicious meal, we ventured outside and we could finally see Turkmenistan. Some thought it would never happen. As we neared the port the sun set over city of Turkmenbashi, it was another awesome sight, but also a reminder of how long we had been trying to cross this stupid sea.

We docked at around 2230, local time, we had lost an all-important hour to the time zone change. We knew we would not be disembarking in the near future, as we had experienced the loading of the vessel. Our judgement was correct, we did not end up getting off that ship until around 0030, this was made longer and more painful by the lorry on the lift, that needed to get us down, broke down

"See Ya Later Shit Lords!"

for a bit. We were finally in the promise land, the place we could only dream about for a week. Little did we know that we had moved from limbo to hell.

We had to convoy around to the customs building to register our passports and our cars like any other normal country. We, being Mikey, Henry, Frosty, and I, handed in our passports first ready to be processed. The man said to wait for five minutes. An hour later the 'German guys' passports had their visa and were paying the cashier lady next to us. We showed our faces to this man again, he said five minutes, another half an hour later the kiwis were now getting processed. (By his timings the man had process ten passports in 10 minutes, that must be some sort of record and he should be due a promotion). It seemed that all the nationalities had to buy their visas together. It eventually got to us Brits. We had to pay the maximum amount for our visas because we were from our Queen's great country. $89 each, this was bearable, a fair price for a visa. There was then a registration fee of $14, this was starting to take the piss but we went along with it. However, this was only the start of the 'wallet-raping', as one kiwi eloquently put it.

Next was the baggage check, luckily no money exchanged hands for this, with the baggage cleared, it was time for the car to be accepted into the country. We met a man who seemed to be insuring our car, as well as adding on yet more pointless expenses, such as $1 for car disinfectant. With this slip of paper it was back to the cashier lady. She added on her 'Random back pocket tax' which gave a total of $178 to pay. We had already spent the majority of our dollars on the visas themselves. I asked if card was taken and, if not, where the nearest cash machine. Both questions were met with an 'X Factor' style cross of arms. They were either really big fans of Simon Cowell or there was no way we were going to be able to pay our way into the country, she had my passport so we had to pay it somehow. As it turned out the nearest cash point was in the city, which was now closed. We had to borrow the remaining cash, to make us up to the magic number, from some very friendly kiwis who had an English uncle who we could transfer the money later.

"See Ya Later Shit Lords!"

You'd think once this was paid the end of the saga was nigh, you'd be very wrong. Many more men, in many more rooms, with many different stamps still had to be visited. We must have all been backwards and forwards to passport control, the ticket office, the cashier, cargo man, and random papers I did not know the meaning about five times each. It was absolutely ridiculous and infuriating. I later found out from Mikey that the main passport officer had a degree in logistics, you couldn't make this shit up. If I had studied logistics for four years and was a part of that cluster-fuck of a system I would personally take myself back to the university that gave me the degree and throw it back in their faces. Some people had theories that the whole process was there to deter tourists, as they are not too keen on them.

The car was finally checked and I was told to pull up to the exit gates, however I was still missing one final tiny slip of paper. Back to the ticket office it was. The lady wanted 4 manat for her to write this note. We only had dollars, she seemed to accept this. Thank fuck. I was ready to go full batshit crazy on this lady. We were finally granted access to this country. We were waiting for the Pug Crawlers to finish their paperwork, the sun was getting ready to rise again. The earth had done half a revolution from the time we had seen the country to actually being allowed in.

It had taken just under one week to get from one border to the other. I had cost nearly $800. With a record breaking wait of nine hours from when the ferry had docked to getting free. It was 0630 on Friday morning when we left and our plan is to drive to Ashgabat, which is a six hours away, rest for a couple of hours, then head up to the Door to Hell (give it a google if you can't wait until the next blog). We are on that road now surrounded by yet more beautiful, but different to anything previous, scenery. This time it is desert and sandy mountains. We have also seen our first camels. The roads are odd, potholes and bumps appear out of nowhere and the side you drive on seems to change far too frequently. One minute you are blatting down the highway on the right side, next you are forced (as the road is not finished) onto the other side into oncoming traffic, with a huge series of lumps and bumps just for good measure. You have to be on your toes, a task made more difficult with no sleep. We have energy drinks though, never underestimate their power. These seem to be the pinnacle of the shit food we have been eating over the past few days, we are all craving a proper meal with identifiable meat.

You might be thinking, why are they pushing on so much when tired? We have no choice. I will level with you, we have booked flights for the 22nd August (a Monday), not realising that you need two working days to load your vehicle on the train for scrapping, meaning we need to be there on the 18th August. Giving us not very long at all. The wait in Baku has screwed over our plan big time, so we have to make up time, if we want to see all of the sights we planned. The Pamir Highway is looking doubtful, even though it is meant to be one of the best bits of the whole trip, it is such a shame and something we really do not want to ditch. We are currently looking at ways round this.

"See Ya Later Shit Lords!"
Chapter 24: Ashgabat and Door to Hell

05 Aug 2016

The road I described in the last blog continued in the same fashion, the potholes, and humped bridges appeared at more frequent intervals. The road condition improved as we got closer to the centre of the capital, as did the amount of gold and white marble covered buildings. For those that don't know much of Turkmenistan, like me before visiting, it is a country that is under a dictatorship and has been since it broke away from the Soviet Union. The previous dictator enforced many ridiculous rules, such as banning algebra, he also named the port city after himself (Turkmenbashi), had a revolving statue that always faces the sun and changed the name for bread to his mother's name. Having read all this we had similar apprehensions as when entering Turkey. The Unknown.[16]

We arrived in Ashgabat at around 1300, having not slept and driven for six hours. We tried to go and get a pizza to lift spirits, as we hadn't eaten anything since the foodstuff the night before. Our plan was to push onto the Door to Hell. However, it turns out that it is very difficult to get money out in Turkmenistan using a bank card that is not from Turkmenistan. (Apparently, there are only four ATMs in the whole country). We didn't have any money to our name,

---

[16] Here are some more detailed facts about Turkmenistan. Detail was a thing we were unable to obtain with the dial-up style internet. The country was part of the Soviet Union for 69 years and declared its independence on the 27 October 1991. Presient for Life Saparmurat Niyazov ruled from 1985 until his death in 2006. He was the dictator that enforced the idiosyncratic policies, mentioned previously. Since the death of Niyazov, the leadership has made tentative moves to open up the country. His successor, President Gurbanguly Berdimuhamedow, has repealed some of the ludicrous policies, such as banning opera and the circus for being "insufficiently Turkmen". There is a lot more information about Turkmenistan online (shock). But it is definitely a country that I would recommend reading a bit more about, because it is so far removed from what is the norm in the western world.

"See Ya Later Shit Lords!"

dollars or manat, after the wallet-raping at the border. After trying at least three different places, we were told the airport was the best place to get money out of a cash point. At this point dehydration was setting in, but we couldn't replenish our water supplies without money, so we got back in the cars and went to the airport.

With the magic manat in our pockets we returned to the city to get that pizza. Whilst eating said pizza we made an executive decision that it would probably be a bad idea to push onto the Door to Hell that same evening, we would inevitably get tired and it would be dark on a road we did not know the condition (spoiler alert it got bad). Having made this decision, out next job was to find a hotel. We didn't have Wi-Fi to compare the best deals or to find a budget hostel, so we did it the old fashioned way. Drive around looking and asking.

We came across the Grand Turkmenistan Hotel, this was a five star place. We originally went into use the Wi-Fi to find a cheaper place, but the internet usage is so restricted by the government, it could barely load the 'G' of Google. We inquired how much it would be to stay there, as you would expect from the name, it was too pricey. The guy behind the desk was offering no discount or other options of cheaper places. So we decided to do one. We had a quick look in their rug shop to see if they were anything like the ones we bought it Turkey. They were much nicer than the ones we had bought, from memory. They were silk and wool blends in much nicer colours. Mikey and I retrieved our Turkish ones from the car to see if the lady would do some sort of rug swap. This was first time we had seen them since Turkey, as they had been wrapped up straight away. We were as disappointed as she was unimpressed with the machine-made rags. The look on her translated, in no uncertain terms, that she would not wipe her arse with these poor excuses of décor.

We left the rug lady, obviously with no such swap secured, and headed for another hotel option. Driving around the city meant that we saw loads of 'spectacular' buildings, they were only there to show how 'amazing' this man in charge is. It was all very fake, and didn't shine a light to the buildings we have previously visited such as the blue mosque, which had real political and spiritual meaning behind

"See Ya Later Shit Lords!"

it. On the other hand the people are all very friendly, not just in the city but across the whole country, more than every-other car that we pass gives us a wave or a toot on the horn. They don't seem too oppressed by their leader. (Who's picture is absolutely everywhere, watching their and our every move).

We eventually found another five star hotel, which was advertised on the map as a 3 star, however the lady behind the desk was very charming, she offered us discount on two twin rooms and was happy to help with our strange Rally requests. (These included asking for a black market tyre shop, something I don't think this lovely lady has been asked before or since). I think we all fell slightly in love with her, and decided to indulge in the rooms for our very last night in luxury (I promise you it is this time).[17] We had been well and truly honey-potted, but we didn't care.[18] We were also introduced to the director (similar to owner but not, as the government owned the hotel), who said he would sort anything we needed. We asked him if he would help us get some new tyres (as the receptionist had not known), he said it would be no problem and we could be driven with a guide tomorrow morning.

Henry and Frosty retired to their luxurious room and went straight to sleep, whereas Mikey and I went downstairs to grab a bit of food and go for a swim and sauna (it had been at two long days without one). On our way to the pool after lots of complimentary food, we bumped into the manager who invited us to sit with him and try the hotel made limoncello. He was also kind enough, once

---

[17] It's not every day you get to stay in a five star hotel in a country that is under a dictatorship. I wouldn't be surprised if Turkmenistan became the next 18-30's destination. A large majority of the people that go on these types of all-inclusive holidays don't know how to do algebra anyway, so there are going to fit right in. We're talking Magaluf, Malia, Zante... Turkmenbashi. You heard it here first, just watch out in the next five years that scene is going to be pumping.

[18] Six months later, I now have no recollection of what this lady looked like, I wouldn't be able to pick her out of a crowd. All I know is that she was very lovely to us and we had been driving in a dessert and been on a ferry for a long time.

"See Ya Later Shit Lords!"

we had chatted and had complimentary dessert, to open up the swimming pool and sauna for us – we had missed the fact that it was closed. This place was awesome.

The outrageously comfortable beds allowed us a well needed nights rest. The morning was filled with breakfast, a visit to the tyre shop with our helpful lady provided by the hotel, and more bartering for rugs to no avail. We were now fuelled with sleep, water and actual fuel ready for the drive to the Door to Hell and eventually Nukus, Uzbekistan.

We were told, by our friend in the hotel, that the only road heading north was fine for a bit and then the condition worsened. He had good knowledge. We started off on a three lane motorway, and thought we would be at the border in no time. Again we were wrong. It deteriorated, allowing us only really to go 50 mph, until the Door to Hell.

There was a smaller 'water crater' marked on the map and it was en route so we went in search of it. However there was no water in it, just a crater with fire at the bottom, a mini Door to Hell. We had no sooner left for the real thing when we were at the turning. There was a group of men gathered in the layby. They were offering to take us up in the jeep for $10 each, but it was rumoured that you could ride motorbikes up and that's what we were hoping for. It was also clear that the sandy roads would be too much for Dominque and the 205 and we would spend most of our time digging her out.

It turned out the motorbikes were un-rentable, but we could hop on the back for 50 manat each. Frosty was practically on the back of one by the time we had agreed. The ride up was incredible. Dipping in and out of sand dunes, with the wind in our hair. The skill of the drivers on the sand was clear, and I definitely would have binned it close to where we started, if we had been left to our own devices. The sight that received us was jaw dropping, I couldn't quite believe what I was seeing. A crater about 50 metres in diameter, with fire in it. It was incredible. Apparently the reason why it is there (for those who didn't do their homework from the last blog) is from when they

"See Ya Later Shit Lords!"

were drilling for oil, the drilling platform fell into the hole and was unrecoverable. It was surrounded by natural gases so they thought they would burn them off to make it safe. It has been alight ever since. It is now a tourist attraction that the government doesn't like people visiting, so much so they disbanded Darwesa as a town all together.

Obviously pictures were taken from the edge but the fact that this was fucking huge hole full of fire meant that it was chucking out some serious heat and you couldn't withstand it for more than a few seconds. Unless you wanted to end up like a half cooked kebab. The ride back down was just as good as the way up. We saw some ralliers who had tried to chance their luck and drive up, they were unsurprisingly stuck. At the bottom our helpful guides were paid and we bid them farewell.

We are now on the road to the border, and Nukus, we have been travelling for 25 miles and already had two flat tyres and uncountable roofbox issues. The tyres we fixed this morning are now all used up. The roads are very shit, only slightly better than the track down to my granny's house (a very niche joke for just my family there). Mikey (who has two more notches on the flat tyre chart, although this might not be fair as the conditions are much worse – but rules are rules) has the dark to contend as well, we long for the boring, smooth, autobahn of Germany. We are sailing very close to the wind with 120 miles to go.

Chapter 25: A Bad Day All Round

06 Aug 2016

We managed to push on last night, without managing to puncture anymore tyres, otherwise we would have been in serious trouble. The roads were just horrendous, we could only average 30 kph as we had to weave around the potholes, brake to make sure the wheels didn't succumb to the huge chasms. We ended up driving mostly on a dirt track to the right of the road, which was slightly better than the poor quality/lack of asphalt.

We were also running low on fuel, every person we asked said a different number as to the distance of the next filling station: 1, 4, 5 kilometres. They were all wrong as it turned out to be around 15 miles until Dominique tasted the sweet benzene nectar. Mikey pulled out of the service station and I said it would be alright to nip down the left hand side of the road, as every other person had been doing that day. Just as our luck would have it, when we got to the roundabout to allow us to get back on to the correct side of the road, it appeared to be one of the police checkpoints. Sure enough the man in uniform blew his whistle and waved his glowing baton, gesturing for us to pull over. Mikey acted dumb (it wasn't hard) as to what had just happened. I thought we would be having to bribe our first policeman. He had a quick look at my flimsy paper international driving licence,[19] even though Mikey was at the wheel, and let us carry on our way.

The roads did not improve until we reached the northern border town, the one saving grace was how amazing the stars in the sky looked with almost zero light pollution. It really was yet another fantastic sight. We decided to use a car park to set up camp for the night.

---

[19] I had bought this from the Post Office for just £5.50 and proved to be a life saver. Even though it wasn't a legal requirement, it looked official enough to mean we didn't have to sacrifice our actual UK diving licences, which are much more expensive to replace.

"See Ya Later Shit Lords!"

It was now 0230 and we knew there would be a long day ahead of us tomorrow. The car park had a strategically placed telegraph pole for the hammocks, it was all we needed. We feel asleep to a chorus of dogs, cockerels (I think this one might have been broken), and many other unidentifiable sounds.

Apparently the place where we camped was quite a big deal in the day time, we woke up surrounded by cars and people milling about some holy building we had not spotted in the darkness of the night before. We packed up our camp in a surprisingly quick time and headed for the border. This was when our day began to become shit.

We passed through the first two passport checks with no problem, we thought that was it. We were out with none of the hassle of getting in. Oh no no no, they had other plans. We had to go inside and go through all of the rigmarole of the entry procedure. We were told we had to pay $11 because we had exited at the wrong place. They would only accept dollars, not even their local currency. Which confirmed our suspicions that it would be going straight in their back pockets. We explained that we did not have any dollars because we had spent them all getting in. Eventually, after threatening to call our embassy, the big boss guy said he would 'cover the cost', how kind of him. Yet more paperwork occurred followed by a very in depth car check. Everything was hauled out, nothing was left without being touched. We were finally clear and ready to head to the Uzbek border, when we met a Mongol rallier from the Ukraine who was having a discussion with the guards. He came over to us and told us to make sure to check we have everything we came in with, apparently him and five other teams were robbed yesterday by the border guards, phones and €4000. We think they had taken 50 manat out of Mikey's wallet, but he can't actually remember how much he had in. It was just another point to add to the list of how shit this country is. The people and the sights were amazing but this is cancelled out by the bureaucratic bullshit and corruption that seems to go on with the officials. (And we thought Ismail was bad). We were glad to be leaving that and the roads, of course.

"See Ya Later Shit Lords!"

We passed through by the Uzbek border with ease and headed to the border town, Nukus, for some food, tyres, and fuel. These simple tasks were not as easy as we first thought. We needed to get out the local currency or dollars to be able to pay for everything. However after a wild and hot goose chase half way round the city, we found out all the banks were closed as it was Sunday, no ATMs took our cards, and nowhere seemed to accept Turkmen manat.

We found a restaurant that had Wi-Fi, again this was still no use. Eventually we asked one of the waiters to come with us to the market to help us try and exchange this Turkmen manat. Everyone in the market carries around shopping bags full of money (because it is 4000 som to one pound) but no one was willing to exchange out Turkmen manat. It was infuriating that they wouldn't take their neighbouring countries currency. Finally we found a guy that did, he gave us 90,000 som. We went back to the restaurant and paid for some food. This wiped out half of what we had just got. There was no way we were really going anywhere today with the little money, and therefore limited fuel and tyres we had.

We have now checked into an Uzbek hotel, with the promise that we will pay tomorrow. We are slowly drifting behind schedule with each decision we make being more stressful. We are going to have some long days driving or come up with some alternative options.

"See Ya Later Shit Lords!"
Chapter 26: Benzene and Tyres

07 Aug 2016

We have written yesterday off as a bad day. Today is a new day. We woke up around 0730, this gave us enough time for breakfast before reaching the opening of the banks, at 0900. A helpful local showed us the way to the bank that accepted Visa cards. We were finally able to get some dollars out to pay for the hotel and the remainder of the expenses of the trip.

I forgot to mention in the last blog but when driving around Nukus, and Uzbekistan generally, we have seen an extraordinary number of Daewoo Matizs on the roads. (This is because they are manufactured here). Dominique was at home. There were Matiz taxis, police cars and various colour combinations imaginable. Every other car seemed to be one. We were hopeful that this would mean it would be easy to get wheels and tyres.

We weren't wrong (for once). The first tyre shop we pulled into had a Daewoo matiz on its sign. We were in business. The guy fixed our three broken wheels from Turkmenistan, all for $10. There was also another guy who was going to get some benzene for us, as the majority of the cars ran on LPG. The guy turned up with random cans filled with benzene and then another guy was siphoning fuel out of his car for us, it was the best way I had ever filled up a car. We also saw a rally car and motorbike pass us when sorting out the tyres, it was Ferghal and Elliot whom we had met in Samsun. This was such a coincidence that we should meet them on this random street in Uzbekistan. We had a quick catch up, they asked us where we were planning on getting today. Our plan was to reach the border, Elliot, who was a fountain of knowledge, reckoned this would be very ambitious and said that Samarkand was a place not to be missed. We changed our plan as we could make up the time. They were heading in the same direction towards Bukhara, we saw them again as we tried to get fuel later on.

"See Ya Later Shit Lords!"

The road heading out of Nukus was again a maze of potholes. Then magically with about 500km to go it opened out into a dual carriageway. This allowed us to reach around 120kph and really get some distance under our belts.

The mood was sombre in the car, Mikey was feeling very ill with a mixture of hay fever, cold and sickness. You know Mikey is ill when he's not waving at the locals and smoking. I had also just found out that our memory card out of one of the GoPros was nowhere to be seen. There was no reason for me to take the card out and it was definitely in there before we passed through the car emptying at the Turkmen border, I wouldn't put it past one of the guards nicking it. I remember seeing one of them playing with the camera. I hope I am wrong and it has somehow dropped out in the car, but that is doubtful. I am absolutely gutted. It had half of everything we have captured of the trip so far. It's such a random thing to take, I don't understand why anyone would take this, and it is worth no money. I just feel as if we have lost a few memories. Money is replaceable, pictures and their meaning are not. Turkmenistan is by far the worst place we have been so far, in terms of badness.

We carried on down the highway which turned into single carriageway, due to road works. We stopped off for dinner at a roadside shack. It had cold drinks and the only thing on the menu was shish kebab. I knew it was fresh, as when I went back to the car to get my sunglasses, they were hauling a live sheep out of the boot of a neighbouring car.

We have now just passed Bukhara, after filling up with fuel. We are about 250km from Samarkand. Mikey is back in the driving seat. I have been driving all day and not had a puncture, I am just waiting for Mikey to get one. It's funny now that we have spares. We are looking for a place to camp just outside Samarkand. This long day will hopefully put us back on schedule after the unplanned rest day yesterday. We hope to make a considerable dent into Tajikistan tomorrow.

"See Ya Later Shit Lords!"
Chapter 27: Not the Best 48 Hours

08 Aug 2016

I'm sorry if the last few blogs have been fairly downbeat and negative. I'm afraid to say it hasn't got any better, if anything our situation is worse than yesterday. This particular blog isn't the one to read if you want to read about how great it is driving across the world. Most of it has been, but our last few days have been shit.

We carried on driving until about 2330 last night, reaching a suitable place to camp, just 20 km outside of Samarkand. Our home for the night was a sandy track just off the dual carriageway. The track was lined with trees so the hammocks were up in seconds, Henry and Frosty were jealous of the swiftness Mikey and I were settled down for the night.

The morning was upon us all too soon, the daylight revealed our campsite was indeed a farm. The locals were milling around, tending to their cattle. We got the inevitable question of 'Where are you from?' These farmers were very kind and gave us a watermelon and some freshly squeezed milk. This B&B wasn't too bad.

During the packing up of camp and breakfast I had a text from Lottie saying that my flight out of Ulan Ude had in fact been cancelled on 4th July (she was looking into how much it would be to change it), as they did not have the correct personal information. This was good in the way that we had no real deadline to get to the finish now, allowing us to arrive on Sunday 21st August and get the car on the train to be scrapped on the Monday and Tuesday. However this was bad in the way that I have unknowingly spent the money that was refunded to me for the cancelled flight.

With the news that we had longer than first thought (about 4 days now, as I still needed to get to India to meet Lottie) we drove the short distance into Samarkand. We were just about to pay to look around one of the famous temples (The name I did not catch as we weren't there for long enough), when Mikey suddenly noticed that

"See Ya Later Shit Lords!"

the $900 he had taken out in Nukus had disappeared out of his wallet. He had been asleep all day and didn't have a chance to split it up. The last place we interacted with wallets was a filling station in Bukhara. They must have taken it whilst we were inside the shop. The list for this country was also stacking up with shit things. We weren't done there though.

After just about getting over the money (which I know I said was replaceable yesterday, but it's still a kick in the bollocks) and the memory card, we went to find Wi-Fi so Mikey could check how much was in his bank account. We got onto the Wi-Fi eventually and we all had an email from the Adventurists which said that there has now been a change of directive on the Mongolian border from big wigs in Ulan Bataar. The directive is to make every team pay a deposit of the same value as it would be to import the car into the country, around $6000. This is will be refunded once exiting the country (doubtful, or it will be a massive hassle). It is to stop ralliers ditching their cars in Mongolia.[20] The Adventurists are currently trying to work a way round this and we should know more once we get Wi-Fi again. Doing the Mongol Rally and not even going to Mongolia seems like we would be missing one of the main reasons why everyone does this trip.

We were all feeling shit again. We got some food and decided to push on towards Dushanbe, Tajikistan. As I said hopefully we can get more info with Wi-Fi. We have been toying with ideas such as driving straight through Russia, going back to Eastern Europe and a final option would be to drive to India to meet Lottie, through Afghanistan, as we did not have the flight to catch. That would be one to tell the grandkids.

---

[20] You might be wondering, as I was, how many cars are actually ditched in Mongolia? There can't be that many? Well I spoke with one of the organisers from The Adventurists after the rally and he said there were at least 70 vehicles in the countryside of Mongolia. I now think it is probably fair enough, if the government didn't want any more ruining their landscape.

"See Ya Later Shit Lords!"

Anyway, we are hoping our luck might change soon. We are driving through the mountain roads in Uzbekistan. I will keep you updated as usual, but you will probably be days behind when this is posted by which time we will be sipping cocktails in Kandahar.

"See Ya Later Shit Lords!"
Chapter 28: Pamir Highway

09 Aug 2016

    We pressed on through the mountain roads towards the border and we were yet again treated to some spectacular views. The roads were not as good as we were expecting so it took a lot longer to reach the border. It was also very stop/start with the police checkpoints, and the issue with the pug crawler's fuel tank line. Mikey was entertaining the group of kids that had gathered, and by entertaining I mean making sure they didn't steal anything out of the car. No one could be trusted now. We gave them some crisps, but they just kept coming back for more shouting 'chippa, chippa, chippa'. The split in the fuel line couldn't actually be sealed, so a hose was shoved through the tear straight into the fuel tank to allow it to fill.

    With the problem fixed and the Uzbek children semi-fed we carried on. Our dinner consisted of bread from one of the roadside stands, which had been warmed by the sun. It went perfectly with the melted butter we had picked up in Samarkand for the sandwiches for lunch and the crisps that were left over.

    We eventually reached the border at around 2030. The Uzbek guards were almost as thorough as the Turkmen guards in terms of wanting everything out of the car. There was only two of them this time, and I was watching like a hawk. I was getting annoyed with how they were still just rifling through bags. They were also sifting through all of the photo albums on our phones looking for porn, something that is banned in either Uzbekistan or Tajikistan we weren't sure.

    After that ordeal, it still took an absolute age to get through the rest of the Uzbek border and then to enter into Tajikistan. We had to pay for medical insurance and road tax. There were so many hoops to jump through. We finally got through around 2300 and headed to Dushanbe to find a hostel for the night. We were wondering around these soviet looking high rise flats for ages trying to find this hostel. We were pointed in the right direction by a Dushanbian and we

"See Ya Later Shit Lords!"

headed into one of the said soviet buildings. The hostel was on the sixth floor and the lift looked dodgier than the men selling currency on the border.

We met some other ralliers who had also been a part of the Caspian Sea fiasco and were making up time themselves. We settled down in the beds at around 0130, they were just what we needed. The much needed Wi-Fi enabled us to catch up with our families, update blogs, and see if there was any update from the Adventurists. Nothing has really changed in that department.

We arose at around 0900, and headed for the Southern Fried Chicken shop across the road. Fast food is something Uzbekistan and Turkmenistan are not famous for, so we were getting our fix. It had nothing on KFC and all made us feel a bit ill, so we swiftly moved on to do our chores before setting off for the Pamir Highway. The chores involved getting water and fuel, as standard, Mikey went to British embassy to see if they could help with an insurance claim for the money that was taken. The woman was highly unhelpful, so we will have to sort that out later in the trip. Frosty and I went to see if we could get money off my MasterCard, although Tajikistan is more developed than the previous two countries it still didn't have cash points that accepted MasterCard.

We decided to get on the road as it was already midday, the money could wait, I don't think we would be haemorrhaging too much cash in the famously baron region of the Pamirs. Just as we left the city the scenery became even more incredible than the day before, and we weren't even at the main event.

We have decided to take on the whole of the Pamir, as Mongolia is now hanging in the balance. As we turned off the main road onto what was officially the Pamir highway the roads were understandably covered in potholes, with shear drops on one side of us and the mountain range all around. It is by far the most picturesque place we have been so far, more so than Austria and Bulgaria. There were kids along the route that obviously know the Mongol rally cars are easy targets for food and general gifts. However, with Mikey's cold, the

"See Ya Later Shit Lords!"

fact that the seatbelt mechanism doesn't allow an inch of movement, and he was trying to reach something from behind, all this meant he wasn't in the mood for the 'chippa kids'. Instead of throwing food at them he threw a snotty tissue. I thought it was quite funny, but Mikey felt quite bad after.

We kept on going, making fairly slow progress because of the roads, we were extremely grateful John had fitted a sump guard as it took an absolute pounding. We were quite worried about the fuel tank though which sits with the same clearance at the back. We drove on until around 1830, we were going to carry on for longer, but we came across the perfect campsite. A slightly raised, flat section of ground just off the main road. It overlooked the fast flowing river that snaked its way through the mountain range. Once again our minds had been blown with the beauty of the scenery that surrounded us.

Hammocks, tents, fire and the shitter were all installed before sundown, a rare luxury for us. It topped the previous campsites again, this road just kept giving. We sat around the fire, cooking dinner, reflecting on the trip so far, looking forward to what lay ahead. We indulged in some star gazing and watched as lightening cracked over the mountains. It was great moment, after the shit few days we had had. Bring on the rest of the Pamir, although I am going to run out of adjectives to describe how amazing this place is. You will have to look at some pictures on our return.

"See Ya Later Shit Lords!"
Chapter 29: Pamir Problems

10 Aug 2016

The campsite was a dream to wake up in, and we were ready to leave at around 0900. Not after a Mikey and Ed river wash special, it was slightly warmer than the Austrian river, the grit that collected in the not-so-fast section we decided to wash, was not a welcome addition. It had rained during the night meaning we had to let the tarp, and everything else we had left out, dry in the morning sun. We had made a last minute decision to put fly sheets and tarps over us last night, this turned out to be very wise indeed.

We set off to tackle the majority of the Pamir today, the roads did not improve so the going was slow as it had been yesterday. We had just forded a river when we noticed the rear right of our car was sagging, although the tyre had not been punctured. That only left the suspension. Once the wheel was removed it revealed a spring that had sheared in two places. There was not a lot we could do other than put the remaining spring back into place and ride with a lower car.

We were looking for someone to weld the bits of spring back together en route and were pointed in the direction of a village where we were inevitably surrounded by the swarm of children, however no tissues were thrown at these guys as we needed their help. There seemed to be a lack of adults, I went in search and came across a lady who was washing up dishes. I had the bits of spring in my hands and gestured a very bad welding action, but she knew what I meant. She led Mikey and me on a merry trip through various passages around the houses to the welding gaff, only to find out that the village didn't have any electricity.

On the return to the car we saw a Lada on wooden blocks, which had some beefy looking springs. We found the welding lady again and asked her if we could maybe borrow them (and when I say borrow I mean take them to Russia and never give back). She didn't seem keen, as she obviously had big plans for this clapped out car. Whilst trying to barter for the springs another rally team turned up,

"See Ya Later Shit Lords!"

The Yurt Lockers, consisting of two Scottish guys, Sam and Lewis. They kindly gave us their last three tennis balls (something we have been meaning to get since Baku as tennis balls are somewhat of rally legend) to put in the springs. This seemed to hold it, and would be enough of a bodge until we could get it properly welded, or get a new spring entirely.

The convoy was now three cars, they were obviously going the same way as us, as there were only two ways along this road, forwards or backwards. Forwards it was. I had swapped into the driver's seat, we had just left the welding lady, and the Tajik Von Trap family, and not more than a kilometre down the road we had another problem.

There was no specifically big rock, or pothole, that we had hit, to our knowledge, but all of a sudden we lost all power, the steering pulled all the way to the right and we were dragged into the ditch.[21] We were moving no further. We both got out to see the extent of the damage. The offside wheel was pointing at 90 degrees to the front of the car. No wheel should ever look like this did. The drive shaft had been ripped from the gearbox, as the rod end from the front suspension arm had completely sheared off and gearbox lubricant was trickling down the road. Mikey got out two cigarettes. I took one, as we both knew that this was more than likely a 'rally-ender'.

The Scots, and Henry and Frosty, turned back to see what was wrong with us. They both confirmed that this was a shit-storm in a teacup. Sam, from the Yurt Lockers, seemed to have the most experience with cars and had a toolbox with a much greater selection of tools than ours. He said it would take a few hours but it wasn't completely un-bodgeable. The sheared pin was stuck in its seated position, so the first job was to remove that. It was very difficult to get at and many different methods were tried. We had brought along

---

[21] I am very glad it was this side that had gone, because if we had been dragged in the other direction. We would have plummeted above 100 metres into the fast-flowing river below, taking our second dip of the day. It would not have just been a rally-ender, but a life-ender.

"See Ya Later Shit Lords!"

a spare front suspension arm for such an eventuality, but only remembered we had it in the roof box until about an hour in to the fix. It would no longer be a bodge but a permanent fix. The other guys had set up shade, music, and water as we all knew we would be here a while. Sam and I set about freeing this pin and changing out this suspension arm. A good six hours later and the job was complete. (I won't bore you with the each and every fine detail).

We have about half the gearbox oil we need, the rear suspension is still broken, and there is still a good thousand kilometres to go of the same roads. The decision was made to turn back, it would have been ludicrous to try and push on further. We bid farewell and thanks to the scots as they headed in the opposite direction to us, forwards along the Pamir, not backwards.

We are on our way back to the campsite we were at last night. We can't be too sad, as the plan after the ferry delay was to miss the Pamir all together, and the fact the flights were cancelled gave us hope that we could get round the whole way. We have done the first day of this unforgiving road and it broke Dominique. She had been pounded for the last week and this was the straw that broke the camel's back. The road well and truly chewed us up and spat us back out.

We have just seen teams heading up the way we have just been, we are covered in dirt and look as if we have been under a car and in the sun for six hours. We got filmed by one of the official Mongol rally filmmakers, explaining our problem. It started to rain, meaning everyone moved off in their respective directions. All we could say to the teams was 'Good Luck'.

Chapter 30: Out of the Frying Pan into the Fire

11 Aug 2016

The mood was still a jolly one, we past our campsite and tried to see how far we could get back to the main road, before it got dark. We wanted to get down off the Pamir as quickly as possible so we still had time to make it north.

Everything was going smoothly until we reached a particularly rocky section of road which we had previously traversed. This time however there was a 'rally-ending' rock that the Pug Crawlers were unable to avoid. This rock snapped their torsion bar suspension clean in two. Frosty compared snapping a torsion bar to the same as breaking two rear suspension springs and then not being able to find the springs to fix them.

Tent pegs with cable ties were used to splint the break, this didn't work. The threaded bar used to hold on their front wheel was the next option. However the threaded bar was welded to another flat bit of metal. We had no means of separating them, the hacksaws had gone with the Yurt Lockers.

Henry and I went up to the nearby village to see if we could borrow one. They seemed to get what we meant when we motioned the actions, but they kept saying 'machina'. We thought they just meant the cars, so we went along with it. We were led to a man's stone house, which had straw for furniture. This man had one better than a hacksaw, he had an angle grinder (hence 'Machina'). It was the dodgiest piece of equipment I had ever used. It would never have even been considered for a health and safety testing back in the UK. The blunt blade wasn't the main issue, it was the fact that it was 'plugged in' by hooking its wires onto the live wires protruding out of his stone wall.

I was in charge of cutting as I didn't want to stand on the metal to hold it in place, as I was wearing flip flops (and had been since Bulgaria). I started cutting and prayed the thing wouldn't electrocute

Henry or me. There were sparks flying out and we quickly realised they were covering his straw interior.[22] Before the whole place went up in flames we took the work outside to finish the job, with our host holding the wire into the wall to make sure it reached. It was a catalogue of errors that you see reconstructed on TV, with the caption 'Look how these morons died'. I'm surprised nothing went wrong, it could have been a lot worse.

With all our faculties intact and the two bits of bar now free, we headed back to the cars. By this time it was now dark, I nearly tripped over countless sitting cows on the way back down. The cars had been moved off the road, it was evident that the executive decision had been made that were camping here for the night, it was not our own choice of course. The attempt to fix the suspension would have to be in the morning. We cooked up our food, discussing options for the remainder of the trip, and then retired to bed.

The next morning was the start of a big day. I had my first 'native' poo (which was an unpleasant experience), but the main issue at hand was to get the suspension fixed on the Peugeot. The threaded bar from the previous night was used as a splint, just like the tent pegs, held in place with cable ties. The car was lowered using the jack, this was the moment of truth. The car just kept sinking, and sinking, until we eventually heard the snap of the cable ties. That was it, we were out of ideas.

The car had to make it off the mountain. The plan was to drive back to Dushanbe, Henry and Frosty had made the decision that the car was too far gone to carry them any further than Dushanbe. For them the rally was over. Even if they had welded the bar it was more than likely to break before they got home. They started ditching stuff, to save weight, to give them a chance to get the pug back to the capital. One lucky local boy had the first pick from the one car 'car boot sale' that seemed to be forming. He got a hat, a crook lock, and a guitar. He obviously went back to his house with his haul, which encouraged more children to join in the auction. A lot of stuff went.

---

[22] This sounds as if we had rocked up at one of the Tajik three little pigs' gaff.

"See Ya Later Shit Lords!"

The European road atlas was an item that seemed to cause a contentious argument between the children. An old man had also come to see what all the fuss was about, he was lucky enough to get the unwanted beers that had been in the Pug since Goodwood. He was in the crouched position on his haunches, a common stance in this part of the world, swigging beer and puffing on a cigarette all at 0900. It was such a funny sight, we had brought binge-drinking Britain to the Pamirs.[23]

We, Mikey and I, have also made the decision to head back to Dushanbe, we are going to try and get our rear spring and 'night sun' headlight (which has come loose through the incessant vibrations from the roads) welded, and fill our gearbox with oil. We are then going to try and push north tomorrow towards Osh. On the way down from the Pamir, the low river crossings claimed our bumper, which had been weaken through the 'Topgear nudges' as we liked to call them. Dominique is now arseless, and looking quite sorry for herself. We had a ceremonial 'chucking the bumper off the cliff'.

Henry and Frosty could only make about 40 kph without the tyres rubbing on the wheel arches and creating a worrying amount of smoke very near the fuel tank. We stuck by them, as they had done with us. It was going to be a long way back. We got about 15 miles into the journey when they ran out of fuel, they had more but the engine wasn't starting. A local truck was heading to Dushanbe and offered to tow them (I don't think Dominique could have handled anymore strain).

Knowing they were heading in the right direction, we have carried on ahead of them so we could try and get everything sorted with Dominique before tomorrow, and the weekend. Mainly the gearbox which is sounding like a box of spanners at the moment. We are going to meet up with Henry and Frosty, at the hostel we stayed in three nights ago, before we say 'see ya later shitlords' for the final time, as

---

[23] And I thought Ashgabat was the next up-and-coming party destination. We have a picture of this guy in his position, which does this description justice.

"See Ya Later Shit Lords!"

they are planning on trying to get the car scrapped and then fly home. I'm sure we will see them back in England, it is a shame we are losing half of the convoy that has been together since Istanbul. We have taken one of their team stickers and hope to take it to the finish line in homage. It will be a lonely continued voyage with out them.

"See Ya Later Shit Lords!"
Chapter 31: "Dollar"

12 Aug 2016

Just outside Dushanbe, on the way back from the Pamir Highway yesterday, Mikey and I found a garage that looked like they could help us with the long list of problems that seemed to be growing with Dominique. We had tried two garages before this, both had no electricity to help us weld the suspension back together, however this one had other solutions.

They did not have the Daewoo rear springs, but they were able to provide some rubber spacers that are more professional than the tennis balls. The night sun headlight was fixed using a larger washer. The power steering belt was fitted and the alternator belt was tightened. The only thing left was the gearbox fluid. They couldn't seem to find a way to fill it, so the noise remained. Other than that, and the bumper, Dominique sounded and ran like a new woman. Her tracking was slightly off, as she pulls more to the left than Jeremy Corbyn, but it is something we can live with as long as the tyres hold out.

Near the Yeti Hostel, Dushanbe, after having the world's worst meal at a steak restaurant that had run out of steak, Mikey and I decided to have one last go at filling the gearbox with oil, under one of the remaining street lamps. We were working away, when a guy who spoke quite good English came over and asked us if everything was alright. Mikey got chatting to him, his name was Alex, and he offered to get us some beers and chat while his kids were playing. While Mikey and Alex went to get some beers I had figured out that it wasn't the internals of the gearbox that was the issue, it was the sump guard that was knocking on the outer case of the gearbox. It had obviously been moved when we replaced the front suspension unit.

Mikey and Alex (who definitely didn't seem like a drug dealer at all) returned with some well needed cold beers. Mikey had asked Alex to write a note in Russian explaining how his money had been stolen, so he could claim it back on the insurance. His kids were still playing around the car and one of them pressed the horn whilst I was

"See Ya Later Shit Lords!"

under the car, it scared the shit out of me, much to everyone else's amusement. With the issue not as serious as we had first thought, Dominique was ready to carry on. We thanked Alex for the beers and his translating abilities and we headed for the Hostel.

Frosty and Henry were already there. They told us how, just after we left them, the truck that was towing them decided to reverse his agreement when he saw benzene pouring out of the Pug[24]. They were stranded in a local village, with no way of driving the car. The rally was very much over for them. They left with the son of one of the villagers on the way back to Dushanbe, without the car they arrived in the country with. I will say no more. It was our last night together so we went up to the local watering hole and had many beers as a farewell. It was reminiscent of how, many moons ago on my birthday, we had met.

The morning brought the final farewells as Mikey and I set off towards Osh. It was weird not driving in a convoy and we felt fairly lonely without the other two. The road north was mainly toll roads which meant they were in quite good condition. The going was still slower than we would have liked as the roads went high into the mountain ranges, the altitude decreased Dominique's performance, and it was second gear most of the way.[25] The slow pace did allow us to take in the breath-taking views once again.

The road also had a number of tunnels. One was marked on the map as 'Dangerous Tunnel' and we now know why. There was little/zero ventilation for this particularly long tunnel. Even with full beams on you couldn't see more than a few metres ahead because of the exhaust fumes. We had the windows up and the vents closed, as

---

[24] The lack of suspension had meant the fuel tank was scraping along the harsh Pamir road, ripping a hole in the tank. Meaning it could no longer be filled and understandably why the lorry had wanted to tow them no further.

[25] The lack of performance was even more evident when you had to crawl past a lorry or a bus that was barely going above walking pace with is bonnet wide open. This is was no make sure the engine could use the maximum amount of the little air that was present.

advised, but we both still started to feel sleepy and light headed by the end. It was well known that if you broke down halfway along, it was pretty much game over. Finally the unforgiving fumy tunnel shat us out the other end into the brilliant sunlight, we were gulping in the fresh air, as if it was a luxury.

We are now just over half way to Osh. Mikey has just been pulled over for speeding, by what looked like the mate of the police officer who was waving the radar gun willy-nilly. They were clearly there to scam money off people. Mikey was playing dumb again (he really has a talent for it) and 'wasn't understanding', until the policeman cupped his hand over Mikey's ear and said 'Dollars', in an almost sexual tone, apparently. Mikey had the ace that was the note Alex had written yesterday. He showed them and gestured that he had no more money left. They either accepted this or got bored of us, as they let us on our way. We have a border crossing and a fair way to go yet so it might be another late one, which might become a regular theme in the next week to make sure we stay on schedule.

"See Ya Later Shit Lords!"
Chapter 32: MISHA

13 Aug 2016

We carried on until we reached the Tajik/Kyrgyz border. Getting out of Tajikistan was one of the easiest processes we have had for a while, the customs documents were handed in, the passports were checked and we were into No Man's Land. We reached the Kyrgyz border and again everything was going fairly swiftly, the passports were checked quickly, but then it came to paying the customs fee for the car. They guy said it would be 1000 Kyrgyz som, I had no idea what the exchange rate was so I wasn't ready to hand this over straight away. It turned out it was $15, but we only had 100 dollar bills (weekend millionaires). Trying to get the change back was a nightmare. It took an hour of bashing on a calculator, the guy disappearing for a while and exchanges of hand gestures, for me to finally pay the charge and get my change back in Kyrgyz som.

Finally we got back on the road and we're going at a fair pace, when we saw a sign that said 40kph. I said 'Why would they possibly have a ridiculously low speed on such a good road', Mikey agreed. We found out, as we hit a massive dip and the whole car dropped, as nearly did our arses. We both looked at each other, laughing. Now we knew.

We pulled off the main road about 20 miles outside of Osh, looking for somewhere to camp, heading up a track past some farm buildings to the top of the hill. With the pug crawlers no longer with us, the hammocks became more difficult to erect. (Some say that's the only reason we were with them). A telegraph pole that had two struts was ideal, and had greater load bearing ability than the Peugeot. (Too soon?) We were both in the hammocks in record time, it was now 0030 and we were shattered.

"See Ya Later Shit Lords!"

The sun woke us up and revealed yet another beautiful vista, which was under darkness when we arrived.[26] Our plan was to get to Bishkek today and find a hostel to stay in this evening. It was about 600km away and we set off around 0830. We made good progress, asking the locals the way as we had lost our main Nav man, Frosty. We noticed that all the local men were wearing these bell/lampshade type hats and we both decided we needed one before we left Kyrgyzstan. Driving through Jalal-Abad led us to a huge street market. We were bound to find one of these hats in there, we pulled over and went to explore.

Sure enough we found the hats we were after. A Kyrgyz guy, who had studied in Germany, told us that the people in the White Mountains wore them to keep the snow off their heads. Pleased with our purchases, we bought some street meat for lunch and headed on our way to Bishkek.

It wouldn't be our Mongol Rally if something didn't go wrong every day. About 20km out of Jalal-Abad, just after we had filled up with fuel, we hit a series of big dips. We came out of the last dip and something didn't sound right. It wasn't the sump guard knocking and we had no drive to the wheels again. We got out to inspect the damage. The same drive shaft as the one that was ripped out, in the Pamirs, had its CV joint in half. Basically, it was not attached to the gearbox, again.

As we were pushing the car across the road into a shady safe area a local guy had spotted us and turned around to see if we were alright. We motioned if he could tow us to a garage. He agreed. He pulled us up a dusty track, getting further into the sticks. We eventually pulled up into this guy's farm settlement. He offered us chi tea and a trough to wash in. This was all well and good but we just wanted to get the car fixed and back on the road. We motioned to say that we wanted a garage (putting our hands over our heads in the

---

[26] This is the photo on the front cover of this book. We really had no idea what lay around us until the sun revealed this view in the morning.

'Pizza Hut' style). He understood eventually and he said/motioned 'This is garage'. We hoped that we hadn't offended him too much, it didn't seem as though we had. He gestured for us to sit and drink tea, smoke cigarettes, and to wash while he went and got his mechanic friend.

Mikey washed his pits in the trough. I washed my, constantly sweaty, feet in what I think was a hand wash bowl only. The mechanic, who was the doppelgänger of Woody Harrelson, struggled to get the wheel nut off to no avail. Our farmer friend went to get us a new drive shaft, he said it was $50 (we didn't see change from our $100 bill). So we were playing the waiting game until he returned.

We were getting worried as it had been a while since our friend had left. We were at his house, so he couldn't have done a runner, he had to come back. (Although I wouldn't have put it past the Turkmen border guards or the Uzbek thieves, they would have screwed over their own grandmother to get $100). The mechanic had downed tools. We then heard the sound of the trusty Nissan that had towed us up here. Of course I never doubted him.

He had returned with the correct size socket and a brand new CV joint for the drive shaft. The socket was put on the nut, but it still wasn't moving even under the weight of two Kyrgyz men. This was becoming squeaky bum time. If he couldn't get this nut off, we weren't going anywhere.

Finally the nut budged, all four of us cheered in celebration. The old, broken, shaft was removed and the new one was fitted, with difficulty but it finally went in. The mount holding the gearbox was also rusted through, this was why the gearbox was touching the sump guard and making the noise I mentioned about before. A new mount was welded together, in the unique way that people do out here by closing their eyes at the exact moment the weld is happening. It is a real skill. A few blinks and welds later, by Woody, and the mount was bolted back in place.

While this was going on, we found out that our friends name was Misha. He communicated with us using different levels of noise,

"See Ya Later Shit Lords!"

one moment he would be using sign language, the next minute he would be shouting. So when we asked his name he was silently pointing at himself and then shouted 'MISHA, MISHA'. Many things were exchanged, we gave him and his children some of the sweets, nuts, and raisins from our ration packs. In return his wife brought us milk,[27] yoghurt, and chi tea. Everyone was happy with their respective gifts.

Finally, it came to the issue of payment, the guy wanted $100 for his labour. We tried to offer him a Cuban cigar instead, but I think $100 will do a lot more for him. It was last of the dollars we had, so we are now back on the search for cash points and banks. We said farewell to MISHA and his family. We were extremely grateful for his help, even if it did cost $200, without him we would still be stuck on the side of the road. We were lucky he stopped and was so friendly.

Dominique is now running better than pre-driveshaft removal. We are still about 500km from Bishkek, which should take us around six hours. It was 1800 when we left, it looks like it's going to be another late one.

---

[27] I thought it was goat's milk, but Mikey told me at the time that he thought Misha was pointing at his wife when she was brought to us. The youngest child was definitely still of the age of requiring breast milk. If offering your wife's breast milk to visitors is the norm in Kyrgyzstan then who are we westerns to turn up our noses. Who knows what we drank, I wasn't complaining. I even finished Mikey's portion, I think he had cottoned on without telling me.

"See Ya Later Shit Lords!"
Chapter 33: All Nighter

14 Aug 2016

It was a late one indeed. So late it became early. The road weaved its way up the mountains, criss-crossing over an aqua coloured river towards Bishkek, it might seem like I describe the same drive through mountains, throughout this trip, but each one has been different and captivating in their own way, whether you were driving it or taking it all in from the passenger seat.

We followed the river upstream which gave way to a stunning lake. We caught the perfect scene, something the camera could not do justice. The sun was setting over the mountains, in the background, the remaining rays of sunlight were shimmering off the lake, in the mid-ground, and the foreground gave us a road that dropped away into a series of hairpin turns.

Beyond the lake, this very road took us up high again into the mountains. It was so high there was snow on the peaks of the mountains. Mikey and I were in shorts and t-shirts from the hot day of driving. We were severely underdressed when it came to filling up the car with a Jerry can. It was absolutely freezing. My hands were shaking holding the funnel, which meant a fair amount of benzene was spilt. With the heating on full blast, we headed down from the mountain range. The worst bit was getting your ears readjusted, as is the custom on an aeroplane. We were shouting at each other, in a similar fashion to how MISHA communicates, until our ears unblocked.

We rolled into Bishkek at around 0230. We were hunting for a hostel in the centre of town, but we couldn't find it for the life of us. Instead we went in search of Wi-Fi which would give us a definitive route. The all night fast food establishments provided us with this service, as well as some well needed street meat. (I think I really need to stop eating this as it really doesn't agree with my bowels. Brussels, is all I will say).

"See Ya Later Shit Lords!"

It was now getting on for 0300, we had lost an hour to the clocks again. Mikey floated an idea that he thought wouldn't go down well with me. His suggestion went something along the lines of 'instead of paying for a hostel for about five hours of usage, why don't we drive to Almaty'. He said he felt like a new man after the nap on the way to Bishkek and was on his second coffee. It wasn't the worst idea I had heard. A 24 hour coffee shop allowed Mikey to get his third fix of coffee and for us to catch up on Wi-Fi, to scope out the route.

Refuelled and ready to go, well one of us, we set off for Kazakhstan. The border was only around 30km from Bishkek, so I caught a few Z's on the way. This border crossing was by far the easiest we have had since Europe. A mere glance at the passports from the Kyrgyz side, lead us to the Kazakhstan border. There were no hidden charges to pay (I sound like one of those insurance adverts from the telly - 'No Win, No fee'), and we were onto the customs check within minutes. I couldn't believe what was going. A quick check by the drugs dog and a bit of banter from the customs guy led us to driving into Kazakhstan.

Mikey resumed the driving to Almaty, as I slept in the increasing uncomfortable passenger seat. He was pulled over for speeding, which was ridiculous as the policeman reckoned it was 30kph on a dual carriageway, the trusty notebook with Alex's (not the drug dealer) note came out and we were on our way again. The familiar pattern seems to be that when Mikey gets pulled over for speeding, it is usually followed by me breaking the car in the same day. (Let's hope not). We arrived into the city for around 0900 and went to another coffee shop for breakfast and some Wi-Fi. I was able to update the blog and we could also both generally catch up on life back home. Something we weren't that keen to do at 0300 the same morning. (Aren't Team GB doing well in the Olympics, after Russia had half their team disqualified).

After a quick look at the monument for Kazakhstan's independence we went to find a police station to allow Mikey to get a police report to claim back the money that was stolen. The maps we were

"See Ya Later Shit Lords!"

using were useless, saying that a hotel and a coffee shop were police stations. We were pointed in the right direction and eventually found one next to the bank. I went to try and get some money out whilst Mikey went to the police station.

Three hours later Mikey returned. I don't know what went on in there but he was clutching the all-important letter in Russian, with an official looking stamp on it. We finally set off from Almaty at around 1500 and stopped at one of the lakes, on the outskirts, for a wash. Imagine a normal Kazakh beach scene with two English men, passing a bottle of Shower Gel between themselves in the shallows. That was us. It was a well needed wash so we didn't care.

On the way from the lake, it was my turn to be pulled over by one of the policeman and their adorable flashing batons. They wanted me to pay a fine of 1000 tenga for not having my lights on, even though it was bright sunlight. The time for acting dumb fell on my shoulders (I wasn't as good at it as Mikey) and the magic notebook came out. They eventually got bored and let me on my way. We are now back on the road again, filled up with fuel and water (Mikey's favourite feeling, apparently). We have about eight hours of driving ahead of us from our wash stop. At home (Cornwall), that's like saying 'Do you fancy going to the beach?'

'Yeah, which one?'

'Scarborough'

The drive will make sure we give ourselves enough time to reach the Russian border tomorrow.

"See Ya Later Shit Lords!"
Chapter 34: Road to Russia

15 Aug 2016

Driving as far as north as we could, into Kazakhstan, was more difficult than we first thought. The road surface was absolutely atrocious and it was made even more difficult in the dark. We were both shattered from the night before and took it in turns to try and sleep in the car, but this was almost impossible. It was like trying to fall asleep on those machines they should have been using to flatten the road. It was alright once you got into the rhythm of having you head smashed against the ceiling, window, headrest, or all three at once.

We got to a point where we both thought it was ridiculous to try and carry on. The road was going to break us or the car. The next turning off the road was taken and the tent, yes the tent, was erected in a field. We were too tired to search for a place for hammocks, so we settled for the tent for only the second time on this trip.

I now know why we use hammocks. The sleep in the tent was largely uncomfortable from the hard, spikey floor, but we were so tired we managed to sleep until 0800. We got back on the road shortly after. It was much easier to pick a path through the potholes and mounds of tarmac that seem to be acceptable here. It was so easy in fact that I was pulled over for speeding quite early on in the day. They had a video and everything, with the speed in the bottom right. I thought we were going to have to pay this time. However, the magic notebook was produced, which said we didn't have any money, in Russian. The policeman bought it for a second then motioned as if to say 'how are you filling up your car with benzene then?' Fair one. That had me stumped. But eventually they got bored again and let us on our way.

The roads did not improve on the way to a nearby town. We were stopping here to get new tyres, some money, food and fuel. The things we need to keep us and Dominique moving. The tyre man was very nice to us, his shop only fitted the tyres but he drove us to a place that sold new ones. We bought three, the lady in the shop (who seemed to laugh at anything) only had the 13" tyres that were bigger than the ones we already have. (If that makes any sense at all?). We fitted two on the back wheels and kept the previous ones to replace the tyres at the front that are rubbing at an alarming rate on the inside. We think the tracking and the general suspension is fucked from all the hits that are taken on a daily basis. The larger rear wheels were interfering with the wheel arches, so they were bent out of the way to stop this. It's great driving a car that is being scrapped. (I won't say it too loud otherwise Dominique might hear and not take us the rest of the way).

The tyre man bought us lunch and let us know that the roads did not improve until Semipalatinsk, a mere 600km away to the north. We didn't need the third tyre we had bought, so we took it back to the laughing lady. She let us swap it for two spare suspension springs, which was very kind of her.

Tyre man was right. We are about 250km away from our destination and we have just passed the 8,000 mile mark on the odometer, which is exciting. Trying to sleep is even more difficult than last night, there are less potholes but the roads have many hidden dips that would test the suspension of any 4x4. The constant up and down motion is becoming tiresome, reminding me of the indulgent food and beer we have had on this trip, as the seatbelt catches my gut. Mikey has now notched up six out of the eight flat tyres we have had overall and one of the night suns has been dislodged,[28] so has been removed. It seems ludicrous that the main road connecting the south and north of a country is so shit. They must at least have some money left over from the Borat film (there it is, the first reference) to spend on it. The scenery is much like Dartmoor, but less exciting. We have

---

[28] We had agreed at the start of the trip that we would try to limit the night driving as much as possible as it would be dangerous. Meaning these lights that we had hooked up to the main beam were more of a novelty that practical. However situations forced us to drive long hours each day and it became unavoidable to drive in the dark. Therefore these Night Sun headlights really came in to their own. We would have been utterly screwed if we just relied on the original lights.

seen just green hills for the last six hours. We just stopped for fuel near a rocky outcrop and that was the most interesting thing we've seen all day. Maybe we have got too used to the stunning scenery of old.

I think the plan is to try and cross the Russian border tonight. We are going to try and get Wi-Fi in Semipalatinsk to see if Mongolia is completely off the cards. If everything goes smoothly tonight, we should be on track for Ulan Ude by Saturday. Fingers crossed. We probably won't make it now I've said that.

"See Ya Later Shit Lords!"
Chapter 35: Mother Russia

16 Aug 2016

We didn't cross the Russian border last night. The decision was made to get a hotel in Semipalatinsk, we had been driving for around eleven hours and had made good time. We'd treated ourselves to the hotel before the long, 3000km, slog to the finish. There had been some word from the Adventurists about Mongolia potentially being back open. However, we have made the decision to carry on through Russia to make sure we are there well in time to experience Ulan Ude before sending Dominique to the big race track in the sky (shhhhh!) and catching our flights.

We had some food and retired to bed at around midnight. The pre ordered breakfast meant we were awake for 0900. After a surprisingly good meal, the road was awaiting us. It was about 100km to the Russian border, according to maps.me (the offline maps we have been using which are properly shit). It tried to take us on an 80km detour, which was obviously ignored, meaning we were there in no time.

We expected this border to be the hardest to overcome, as we had such difficulty obtaining the visas. We were out of Kazakhstan with no issue at all and we were soon onto the Russian side. I thought 'Here we go, this is where the eight hour wait occurs'. Wrong again. A check of the three passports (Dominique's included) and a quick rifle through our belongings, (When I say rifle, I mean a glance into the car, nothing as obscene as what occurred in Turkmenistan) and we were taking pictures under the Russian sign before we knew it.

We are very grateful of the long, straight and more importantly smooth roads that Russia has to offer. It means some serious mileage can be put down in the next few days. With the straight long roads comes the monotony of the same scenery, but I will take it over the littered potholes any day. However one part of woodland provided a huge amount of amusement for me, not so much for Mikey.

"See Ya Later Shit Lords!"

I was told that I had to pull over at the next set of discrete looking trees, by Mikey. He needed a sit down toilet, rather than the more convenient stand up toilet, urgently. The service station was too far away. I left him to take our collapsible toilet seat and some toilet paper into the woods. What returned was a very unhappy looking shell of a man, demanding wet wipes immediately. I had predicted what had happened as a similar fate had occurred to myself, during a dry run, in the Pamir's. The toilet seat had collapsed leaving the occupant (Mikey) to fall into, and hence be covered in, the very object he had just deposited. A good five to ten minutes later, Mikey returned, I think most of the damage was now under control. I couldn't stop laughing. He said that 'Anyone who has just fallen into their own shit, should be treated like a king for the rest of the day'. Which is fair enough.

We carried onto another fuel station, as the fuel gauge was telling us we were nearly empty, even though we had just filled up. We thought there was a leak, in reality the fuel gauge is broken which is a bonus. I bought Mikey a huge Russian flick knife, partly because he had lost his somewhere in Turkey, mainly because he had just fallen in his own excrement. I was treating him like the pooey king he was.

We are back on the beautifully flat roads and we are looking for somewhere to camp, just north of Barnaul. This will leave us with about 2250km to do in the next three days. We are still on track for Saturday and we are praying nothing goes wrong on the way. I will be avoiding the folding toilet seat in the meantime. The mood is a long way from what it was a week ago, we are excited to have nearly completed this epic adventure. (Something is definitively going to go wrong now).

"See Ya Later Shit Lords!"
Chapter 36: "Fifty Bucks"

17 Aug 2016

We made good time to Barnaul where stopped for something to eat at Burger Club (I have broken the first rule already). Refuelled, we headed out of the city towards our planned campsite. We were making good time, although maps.me was still saying it would take another hour and a half with 50km to go. This seemed ridiculous, we were going way quicker than that. (We need to stop making these wild statements, the opposite happens every time). There was a funny noise coming from the same left front wheel with the previous issues. There was nothing obviously wrong when we stopped, the wheel was changed just in case, but there was still something wrong with the tracking. If you let go of the steering wheel for a second the car violently and dangerously veers off to the left into potential oncoming traffic. It was far from ideal. It had been doing this slightly before, but it was much more prominent now. We carried on in spite of this, we couldn't turn back or take it to someone as it was 0030.

We took the turning off the main road that maps.me was suggesting. It took us onto the, all too familiar, potholed roads through a small village. This then became a farm track which cut its way through high grassed fields. I expressed to Mikey that this definitely couldn't be the main route that everyone takes between these fairly large cities. The first part of the track was solid and easily navigated. We then reached a particularly muddy part that had been chewed up by a tractor. The track was full of murky water. I decided to go for it. I floored it and predictable came to a halt in the middle of the quagmire, wheels spinning, beached. I blamed Mikey and the maps, but admittedly I could have chosen a better route.

I was driving so it was Mikey's job to get out and push. Still nothing. We tried putting anything we could under the wheels to get some traction. No movement. We tried digging out the mud from underneath the car. This was useless as well, as it was that sort of mud that sticks to everything. We were both wadding around in mud

"See Ya Later Shit Lords!"

halfway up ours legs by this point, arms covered. She wasn't going anywhere. It was now 0130 and there was no chance there would be anybody coming along this road. (Maybe ever!) We had inadvertently found our campsite for the night. The tent was set up, on a suspiciously looking hard path that is probably used to avoid said mud pit, the light would have surely revealed this to us. We positioned the tent on the makeshift road to make sure any passer-by would have to wake us up to get through and consequently tow us free. This was not how either of us had imagined our night would end. Sleeping the middle of a field, covered in mud.

No such luck with our theory that people would be queueing to get passed us, knocking on the tent to move our car. We were also right next to a train track, which had given us many false hopes of freedom last night. There was a track that ran beside it. Mikey went in search of someone who could tug us off the mud bank. My job was to disassemble the tent, pack everything up, and wait for the very slim chance that someone may come along. I was distracted by the many mosquito bites that had appeared from last night's antics, they were most likely attracted by the mud that was now covering everything.

Mikey returned, surprisingly quickly, in the passenger seat of a massive truck. The kind we usually get stuck behind on the main roads. This time it was our friend. A tow rope was attached and within seconds we were pulled out of the mud to freedom. We thanked our lorry friend and packed up the car. I removed the sump guard, as it was caked in mud and had been making a noise when we changed gear since the Pamir's. We would hopefully no longer need it. (Famous last words). This venture subsequently covered me in even more mud, providing more bait for the mosquitos.

We carried on down the track we had attempted last night, the daylight did indeed revealed paths around the huge mud puddles. We had made it onto a semi acceptable road, just beside a train track when we heard the familiar noise of the CV joint, on the drive shaft, not doing what it should. There was no drive again. This was starting to become fucking annoying. We had managed to break down on a

"See Ya Later Shit Lords!"

well frequented truck route, one was flagged down and we explained that we would appreciate it if he could tow us to a garage. He obliged, but only as far as the main road. I think he must not have been going in the same direction as us. Another car, full of a family, was hailed and they agreed to tow us the rest of the way to the nearest garage.

This is where we are now, and have been for about two hours already. They have taken the drive shaft off, and Dominique has just had a power wash as she was inevitably covered in mud from the previous night's antics, we also took the liberty of using the jet wash on ourselves. We have the same problem as when we were in Kyrgyzstan. However, after many hilarious translations using our Google translator app (one being 'use your mother instead'), they can't seem to find the replacement part. We told them that the part had already been replaced about four days ago. They said 'how much did you pay for it?' We replied 50 dollars. They all burst out laughing. However, when we asked them how much this part would be now they started talking amongst themselves 'something in Russian, Russian, FIFTY BUCKS, Russian....'. So it looks like it's going to be the same amount.

With our money in their pockets the guy has been to the next city over and has been ringing around everyone. This could be our rally ender if they can't get the part today. We have been looking at options of transporting the car to Ulan Ude and scrapping her entirely, both are going to be very expensive. We are currently waiting to see how it plays out, we could be joining our friends, the Pug Crawlers, when we are so close to the end. It is a real shame and a decision we won't take lightly.

"See Ya Later Shit Lords!"
Chapter 37: She Lives!!

18 Aug 2016

The guy, who went to get the part, finally returned after we had been sitting/sleeping in the sun, waiting. It turned out he had driven around 100km to get the CV joint. It was fitted swiftly which meant the issue of the bill. He said the part was an 'original' and he wanted us to pay for the fuel that was used to fetch the part as well. That day ended up costing us two thirds of the original cost of Dominique. We had got to the garage at around 1130 and we eventually drove onwards at 1800, after the garage guys had taken pictures with us. It will probably go on his wall with the caption 'English idiots who we ripped off'. We didn't have any choice.

We pushed on until around 0030, again, to try and claw back the many hours we had lost that day. Eventually, enough was enough and we thought it would be better to get some sleep. The scene of turning off the motorway to find somewhere to camp was a very common one now. We found an inlet into a field of corn which was just big enough for the tent (no trees for hammocks, we only had one more night to use them) and for Dominique, who was facing outwards just in case we had to make a quick escape from an angry Russian farmer.

No such farmer disturbed us and we were woken by our alarm at 0700. A big day of driving needed to happen in light of yesterday's events. Everything was going swimmingly for the first four hours of the day, this was until the now fateful time of approximately 1130. We were in the city Krasnoyarsk, just coming off a dual carriageway, to join another, to bypass the city. A left handed U-turn was needed. As we rounded the turn we heard the dreaded 'clunk clunk clunk' and we knew CV joint had gone again. We pushed her to a nearby car park to see if it was definitely the same problem. It seemed to be working in a straight line when we tested it in the car park. There was a garage just 200 metres from our location, according to maps.me (it didn't actually turn out to be a police station as we were expecting). We tentatively drove Dominique round to get her looked at once again. The sound was still there, but not constant on the short journey. What was wrong with this car? It was infuriating.

Sure enough, once the mechanics had taken the drive shaft out, they showed us exactly the same problem we had seen three too many times now. The parts guy of the garage, and boss, was ringing around to see if there were any drive shafts in the city. It was almost as if we were in Mongol Rally Groundhog Day. There was a part available but according to the dodgy Google translate it might be 'risk'. We had a huge decision to make. How much more money could we throw at this? How much would it be if we decided to dispose of the car and end the rally? What were the other transport options available to us? All of the above had to be considered as well as the fact that we had just forked out an extortionate amount of money for a part that had only lasted a day. The same thing could occur to the most recent joint, if we could get hold of it.

We weighed up our options. A flight to Ulan Ude was too expensive. The train was the cheapest option, but we would have to try explain, and then pay for, the car to be scrapped. The only real choice was to get the part and carry on.

We were driven by the boss and his mechanic (who, according to one of the locals who was also getting his car fixed, looked remarkably like Barrack Obama. The local's observation, which took an age to convey to us through Google Translate, wasn't too far off the mark, if you squinted), to the parts shop. Barrack made sure it was the right fit, we paid the parts guy (which is why we were made to come along, to make sure we knew the boss wasn't ripping us off) and then we headed back to the garage. Barrack and another mechanic, who had a constantly pained look on his face, fitted the part. Mikey and I paced up and down in the waiting room at almost the same rate as the athletes in the Olympic walking race that was being broadcast from the TV in the background.

The car was back together by 1500, we hadn't actually lost that much time. We paid for the labour and bid the team farewell. As we

"See Ya Later Shit Lords!"

were turning left out of the garage, Mikey jokingly mimicked the noise of 'clunk clunk clunk', no sooner had he said it, the noise had returned for real. Dominique was back on the ramp and after more inspection the problem was finally solved. It wasn't the CV joint that was the issue, it was the gearbox mount that was bodged by MISHA's mechanic all that time ago in Kyrgyzstan. It wasn't tight enough, so every time we turned left it would pull the drive shaft from the gearbox. The cheapest option would be to carry on to Ulan Ude and avoid turning left. Somehow I don't think even we could pull that off.

The boss was back on the phone now looking for this part. Luckily this one was around as well. However it was on the other side of town. Mikey and I were once again driven, but this time in the Boss's swish Infiniti SUV, his girlfriend was also along for the ride. Mikey and I felt like their children sat in the back, we were shattered from the constant driving, and both of us fell asleep during the 40 minute drive. We were awoken by our new Russian parents when we arrived. The part was once again bought, and we headed back to the ranch. There was a lot of traffic on the way back, we were getting restless so 'Mum' had to give us a juicebox to calm us down. (I wish, there was no interaction with our Russian mother due to the increasingly annoying language barrier)

Anyway, we eventually got back to the garage for the third time (if turning left counts as the second), the part was fitted, we paid for the labour and we were bidding farewell to everyone again. We noticed they collected coins, so we gave them the currency from most of the places we had been in Europe as a thank you, it also cleared out the door handles where they have been collecting for nearly five weeks.

We thought that was it, Burger King was beckoning as we hadn't eaten all day. Fate had other ideas, on the way there was another wobbling (which is very difficult to translate into Russian) coming from the infamous left wheel. We swung her around and pulled back into the garage, for what was the fourth time today, with a sheepish look on our faces that didn't need translating.

"See Ya Later Shit Lords!"

Barrack had Dominique up on the ramp again. It seems as if the replacement CV joint (the only one for miles remember) had been broken in the short period of time between driving with the old gearbox mount and the new mount. It really was squeaky bum time now, they kept the garage open just for us. This is where I introduce 'The Doctor' (dubbed by Barrack), he didn't have a sonic screwdriver nor a stethoscope. We had seen him around during the day, working on other cars, as he was smashing bits of metal into submission (the beauty of the craftsman). His heavy hands from early were now in delicate mode. He was only bloody rebuilding the CV joint using the parts from the old one.[29]

Mikey and I were back to the Olympics, popping our heads into the workshop to see how our patient was doing. We were given a shake of the head, by Barrack, as if any distraction could lead to the drive shaft bleeding out on the operating table, along with our hopes of finishing with Dominique.

Half a volleyball match later and a walk to the recently discovered 24 hour supermarket, the Frankenstein drive shaft was complete. We returned from the shop stuffing pizza in our faces to see Dominique back in one piece. She was given a quick test run, the vibrations had been ironed out. We were back in the game. Again.

It was 2130 by the time we left. The guys were glad to finally see the back of us. Dominique is running as smooth as ever. Let's see how long she lasts this time. We have just stopped off at Burger King, refuelling for the long night ahead. We are planning to drive the 19 hours straight through. Meaning we should have finished the Mongol Rally by 1830, tomorrow. That thought to me is excitement, relief and sadness all rolled into one.

---

[29] It was like watching the Hulk just smash up a city and then thread the needle required to sew his shirt back together.

"See Ya Later Shit Lords!"
Chapter 38: The Final Curtain

19 Aug 2016

We have just been driving. Nothing too exciting has happened in the last extended day. We set off from the Burger King at around 2200, as I may have mentioned in the last blog. This was the long slog. We just wanted to get to the finish. Maps.me said it would be 19 hours of driving. We were up for the challenge.[30]

Mikey took the first stint, whilst I slept. We swapped at around 0530 and I carried on until around 1330. We were being gentle with Dominique, she had had a long innings and we just want her to take us to the finish with no more issues. She has been an absolute trooper.

The afternoon saw us reach Lake Baikal. We thought it would be rude not to stop and have a swim. Our last nature wash. We took it very easy over the bumps which lead to the beach, we weren't breaking down again with just 300km to go. The lake was predictably freezing, but we were able to stay in long enough to wash our pits and bits. This was greeted with bemused looks from the locals.

We sat in the sun and cooked our remaining boil in the bags. The energy for the final three hour push to the finishing city of Ulan Ude was going to be crucial. The beach entrance was negotiated with great care on our exit, and searching for Dominique's final ever petrol station. It felt odd and kind of sad that we would never put fuel in Dominique again, something that was a regular occurrence and had become second nature to us. It was the sign that the trip really was drawing to a close.

Mikey swapped into the driver's seat with around 200 km to go. Our original plan was to head to the official finishing line tonight, we made the decision to head straight to the hotel and complete the

---

[30] The maps.me estimate was always hugely ambitious, so we knew there was more in store for us than the 19 hours quoted.

"See Ya Later Shit Lords!"

ceremonials in the morning. (Obviously for better photo opportunities in the day). Just outside the city the roads became extremely potholed again, we weren't going to get off that easily. It was dark and much harder to pick a route when you have the persistent full beams of the stubborn oncoming traffic.

Mikey was doing his best but each hole we hit felt as if it was going to snap the chassis in half and that would be the end. However, our thinking was, with each kilometre we gained the less distance we would have to be towed. Therefore the more likely we were to actually finishing. We didn't get off with nothing. When I say we, I mean Mikey, got another flat tyre. This brought his total on the trip to seven, with mine being one. (We won't mention the other charts we had running). It wouldn't have been right if everything had gone smoothly. We changed the tyre with what we hoped would be the very last time.

The big city lights loomed. We were willing Dominique to take us in. She obliged. As she had for the majority of the adventure. Passing the Ulan Ude city sign meant we had reached our destination. We had finally made it. We have driven for 24 hours straight through. It was such a weird feeling. We had completed what we had set out to do. It was a sensational feeling.[31]

We are just in the hotel now, ready to go to a nearby revolving restaurant/bar for some food, beers and shisha. (The only fitting way to end it seems). We will then retire to bed for what I imagine will

---

[31] During our 24 hour driving mission we did complete a move that we were surprised that we hadn't tried sooner on the rally. This was what I like to call the old 'In-Car Switch-a-Roo'. To explain, if the title is not enough of a giveaway, it involves swapping the driver of the vehicle without stopping. This occurred on a flat section of straight road. I was in the driver's seat and shuffled all the way forward in my seat. Mikey sort of worked his way behind me, with his legs either side of me as if I was giving him a piggy-back. Mikey then worked his foot towards the pedal, and slowly took over control of the accelerator. Once this was established, he took the steering wheel, as I vacated. It all happened very swiftly and smoothly, without incident. Maybe it was only a thing we could pull off once.

be a sleep that will stretch long in to tomorrow. I will let you know how the finish goes and give you some stats on the trip tomorrow.

"See Ya Later Shit Lords!"
Chapter 39: Officially Finished

21 Aug 2016

We have officially finished. We stayed in the Hotel Ulan Ude last night and awoke today at around 1300, catching up on some well needed sleep after the previous day's mammoth drive.

The main event today was actually getting to the finish line, situated at Altan Hostel. A stone's throw (6km) from our hotel. Dominique just had to make it there and survive long enough to get on the train the following day. We were so excited to actually start the process of bringing the last five weeks to a close. The launch at Goodwood seems such a long time ago.

We turned up at the hostel, having got lost for a final time only to realise it was literally behind us with a massive great sign saying 'Mongol Rally Finish'. We pulled in and there were already about four cars there, the kiwis from the ferry and another team we had met in Dushanbe. That was only their cars though, there wasn't actually anyone around. It was a bit of an anti-climax, if I'm honest. But I don't really know what I was expecting,[32] which is a statement that can traverse most of the experiences we've had in this trip.

I suppose that's what it is all about. I don't want to go into the cliché of how I found myself and I am now a spiritual person, because I did a thing, but there has definitely been a change in how I generally view the parts of the world we have been lucky enough to pass through. For a start I have a greater understanding as to where the countries are. The main thing I would take is how friendly the people are and how much they want to show what their country has to offer, be it scenery, food, and/or culture. This good-nature has been a constant in almost every country. However I believe our naivety has been quashed by the few events we experienced where

---

[32] Strippers, free beer and an oversized confetti cannon - is exactly what I was expecting.

people are very willing to rob you blind. It is an eye opening experience in both aspects.

Enough of that bullshit. We wondered into the bar to see if there was anyone around to physically let us finish. We saw the registration table and headed over. We were greeted by someone from the Adventurists. He said 'Oh have you just arrived?'

We said 'Yes, we are here to finish the Mongol Rally.'

The guy replied, taken a back as if it was a shock we were actually there 'Come and sit down and we will get you booked in, Congratulations.'

That was it. We filled in the paperwork and we were handed our veteran's card and some beer tokens. We were the 68th and 69th (Mikey enjoyed this) people to finish.

We had our free beer and then took Dominique out to the finishing podium. Mikey drove her on, I didn't think she was going to make it, but there was still fight in the old girl. We asked someone from another team to take some photos of us. I got Mikey and Dominique soaked with champagne. I think this is the feeling I was looking for at the finish line. It felt right.

Next came the unpacking of the car. We found so much stuff that we had lost under all the shit that had accumulated during the trip. We hadn't repacked the car for a good week as it had either been broken or we had just been driving to make up the time. Everything we didn't want went in a pile for charity. So much went, Mikey was brutal, but it had to be done as I am a bit of a hoarder, until we were only left with one big bag and one hand luggage sized bag each. Plus a communal bag of items we couldn't leave, which will go back to the UK with Mikey.

With everything gone it was time to head back to the hotel, before some food. We got about a kilometre from the finish hostel towards our hotel when we heard a pop. It was my second flat tyre of the trip. Typically, we had just chucked away the spares and the

"See Ya Later Shit Lords!"

socket set,[33] so I swung her around and back to the finish we went, pretty much driving on the rim of the front left. That bloody front left. We couldn't have a day without an issue remember.

Eventually, after changing the wheel, we arrived back at the hotel. We have the Olympics on again, still the same three sports they keep repeating (handball, volleyball, and basketball) and we are just about to head out for some food and then to our local. The revolving bar. Mikey has his flight in the morning and it is my job to drop Mikey off and then take Dominique to the car equivalent of the electric chair.

---

[33] This is what was left of the socket set. During the unrelenting terrain of potholes and undulating tarmac the roof box was barely clinging on by the end of the trip. It had sorted of moulded itself around the roof bars and was held on by a number of ratchet straps. This also meant there were lots of holes and cracks that formed in the shell of the box. It became less of a Tardis and more like a sieve. Anyway the socket set box had also been battered throughout the journey. At random intervals of particularly bumpy driving we would hear the metallic sound of sockets, spanners, and heads to screw drivers escape through the holes in the roof box and bounce down the road. By the luck of the Gods (and before we decided to move the toolbox into the cabin as a preventative measure) the only socket and spanner that didn't worm their way free was the 17mm. This was the size of the nuts on the wheels, if these had disappeared there would have been no way to change the abundance of flat tyres that plagued us.

"See Ya Later Shit Lords!"
Chapter 40: Dominique's Eulogy

22 Aug 2016

Today was a day we had to say goodbye to our trusted travel companion and friend. Dominique. She gave Mikey his last ride, when I drove him to the airport this morning. I had until 1300 before she had to been given up. I went back to bed for a bit before the separation and tears.

I drove Dominique down to the hostel I am staying in for the next couple of nights (Clean hostel, which is clean as the name would suggest). I dropped my bags off and then it was time for the final drive to the railway freight station. She was performing like a dream, without all the weight she had lugged here. She had a new lease of life, as if she knew what was coming and was showing me she still had it. She was like a dog that gets excited for a walk, until they realise they are going to the vet instead. This time there would be no magic medicine, Dominique was being put down.

I was following the directions the Adventurists had provided. However they seemed to take me onto a sandy track on the other side of the railway from where I was meant to be booking Dominique in. But I didn't really care, we were both enjoying driving in the sand so much, I just kept going for a bit even though I knew I had gone wrong. The sand meant the steering went lighter and you could really kick the back out and drift through the corners. Who was I to deny Dominique her final pleasure? It was a great moment. I had the similar feeling of excitement when I had first picked up Dominique in Durham all those weeks ago. Just man and machine in perfect harmony.

I eventually realised that I was going to be late and Dominique would not be going anywhere without paying an extortionate amount of money (you'd probably think we were used to that by now). I swung her around and took her to the Mongol Rally graveyard, there

"See Ya Later Shit Lords!"

were about 40 cars already there. We made it about 41. The paperwork was filled out, the last painstaking process. Then that was it. I gave her a tap on the roof as if to say thank you. She had her issues but doesn't everybody. She had made it, even though it was touch and go at some points as to whether we would have to scrap her and carry on using another mode of transport. She had one of the smallest engines, 0.8 litre three cylinder engine, but she had done all the things the big boys had done. Many people thought she wouldn't make it, neither did we at some moments, but she has defied all the odds. She completed 10,127 miles through 20 countries on some of the toughest roads in the world. Thank you again.

Here is everything that Dominique had wrong with her during the trip. It is in no particular order, just how I remember them. The rear right suspension spring sheared in two places, bodged using tennis balls and rubber Daewoo discs; bumper fell off in the Pamirs, launched down the side of a mountain; front left suspension had a sheared rod end which consequently ripped out the drive shaft along with gearbox lubricant, took six hours to fit the new spare we luckily brought with us; CV joint broke for the first time in Tajikistan, towed by MISHA for his friend to fix it in return for a fair amount of money, he also noticed the bracket hold the gearbox in place was rusted through so welded a new bit of metal in its place; CV joint broke for the second time in Russia after being stuck in the mud, replaced by an 'original' part which we think they just wrote the price on; CV joint broke for the third time in Krasnoyarsk, a day later, a much more professional garage helped us get a new one and found the source of the real problem which was the welded gearbox mount, we were not actually ripped off by these guys (a first for everything).

We went through 10 tyres, mainly due to the fact that the two front tyres were pointing inwards after all of the pothole hits, but I like to think it was Mikey's driving as he racked up 7 (we won't mention the Gears Ground chart); the fuel gauge didn't work; the fuel tank couldn't actually be filled all the way to the top as there was a hole which we noticed before we set off, one of us had to make sure

"See Ya Later Shit Lords!"

the Mario pump attendants would stop before it all started pissing out; one of the original lights didn't work; one night sun was dislodged due to excessive vibrations; the roof-box had countless holes in it and was held on by two ratchet straps and the fact that it had moulded around the roof bars; the wheel arches had to be flared as the tyre shop only had tyres that were two sizes too big; the bonnet catch broke; the sump guard had to be removed as there was so much mud and it was interfering with the gearbox; the power steering belt snapped on the second day, wasn't replaced until Tajikistan; alternator belt had been loose and squeaky since we left. Don't even get me started on the fucking seat belts.

There must be more that I have forgotten. But apart from the above everything went smoothly. Not many people can say they have driven their first car over 10,000 miles in five weeks to Siberia. We couldn't have asked for anything better (well maybe). She has now gone to the racetrack in the sky. Hopefully she is using her Korean charm and flirting with the American Muscle cars, punching above her weight as usual.

RIP Dominique (2002-2016)

'The most stubborn car I have ever met.' - Ed Blackwell 2016

'This underdog went above and beyond.' – Mikey Parlby 2016

All that is left for me to say is some Thank You's. Firstly to our sponsors: Fletcher's Solicitors; The Rotary Club; Milford Farm; Graspan Frankton; GoFilmYourself; Polyflor; Advanced Engravers; and Ben Murphy's Face. All have been fantastic in supporting our adventure, without them we wouldn't have been able to make this happen. All those who have donated to our charities: The Back Up Trust; The Max Levene Trust; and Cool Earth, the page is still open so if you are reading this, I hope your next move is to the donation page if you haven't already. [34]

---

[34] There is more detail on both the Charities and the Sponsors in the following pages.

"See Ya Later Shit Lords!"

Finally, to you the reader thank you for coming along on this journey with us, it has been great to hear the feedback, it gave some meaning to actually writing these. I promised you at the start that it would incredible and unmissable. I don't think Uncle Ed was wrong.

Until next time. Over and Out.

"See Ya Later Shit Lords!"

Epilogue

Seven months has now elapsed since we completed the Mongol Rally. Meaning it is just over a year since Mikey and I clicked 'Submit' on our applications. I believe as if a sufficient amount of time has passed to be able to reflect on the experiences we shared, all over the world, in the summer of 2016.

I have similar feelings to those present when we rocked up to the finish line hostel in Ulan Ude. I still don't fully comprehend the sheer extent of the achievement, even after half a year of reflection. We drove 10,000 miles over a third of the world's surface in a shitty car. This is a statement that never fails to shock people that have never heard of the Rally before. However, I just think of it as that 'road trip' Mikey and I went on in the summer. We just took each day at a time. Fixed things if they went wrong, decided which river to wash in, chose where to hang our hammocks and occasionally, talked our way out of a police fines. These were just some of the things that were our immediate concern. We never really considered the wider picture.

Compiling this collection of blogs into this book has been vital in trying to condense those five weeks into a tangible picture. Each chapter allows me to delve deeper into a memory that would have otherwise been forgotten had I not written them down. Which is why this is book is probably most important for Mikey and myself (and Henry and Frosty to an extent) and it is a bonus if anyone else happened to like it.

This wasn't just about us though, as we were also raising money for our three charities. We managed to raise over £2000, a quarter of this will go to the Cool Earth charity and the remainder will be split between The Back Up Trust and the Max Levene Trust. Meaning a large amount of the cost of Max's new wheelchair will be covered. More detail about each of these charities can be found in the appendices that follow.

"See Ya Later Shit Lords!"

Mikey is now in a full time job, working in Bristol, and I am currently holding down temporary employment before moving to Edinburgh later this year for my full time job. This, in a way, makes me sad. I understand how lucky we both are to be employed, but it means we are coming to that strange cross-over period that occurs in in many young people's lives. There is a sudden switch from having all the time in the world with relatively little funds, to then having enough money to go on adventures but your free time takes a turn for the red depths of overdraft. Once your summer travels, now adventures you only have time to day-dream about. Maybe this is a morbid perspective of full time employment, but I'm sure there are plenty of people that think this way.

This viewpoint is why I am so happy that Mikey and I cashed in on the time we had, by planning and undertaking this trip. Many people would have been sat at a desk dreaming about what could have been, whilst Mikey and I grabbed the bull by the horns. With this in mind, I would encourage you subvert the norm. If you have the time, scrape together what money you have and go see the world. If you have the money, what are you waiting for?

I can understand that not everyone can simply disregard work or magic up some money. What I would say is that if you have the opportunity to experience other cultures, or do something you wouldn't normally do, or challenge yourself, then do not hesitate because you may regret it in later life.

The whole trip really was, and still is, an education that simply cannot be taken from a textbook or a lecture, you have to be present. This type of learning allowed me to enjoy the highs and accept the lows that are the nature of such an endurance event. The main thing I gained as a result of the trip is a greater empathy with the people from all those amazing cultures. We were able to gather a brief snapshot of how they lived, amalgamating the desirable aspects into our own way of living, whilst understanding why they tolerate some of the less desirable ways of life. For example, when we were sat in the eight hour queue to cross the Turkish/Georgian border, no planning or frustration is going to make the queue go any faster (although incessant horn honking did seem to work in some cases), you just have to accept this fact, as the locals have done for the whole of their lives. As we travelled further east, away from Europe, it was clear that the local people have thrived in their environments for thousands of years, with a fraction of the privileges available in the western world, yet they seem to be more content with their lives. They do not feel the need for constant gratification of people that they are only friends with on social media. Their happiness is grown out of the face to face human interactions.

Meeting new people in different cultures, whether they are good or bad experiences, is only going to enhance further interactions in the future. I have become more confident in knowing how to handle situations, knowing when to have my guard up and when to relax it, this came through the many exchanges we had.

Do you want to be the old person in a retirement home sat on a pile of cash he has saved for the whole of his life having only ever known his home town; or do you want to be the old person who has a wealth of stories about their adventures, people they have met and cultures they've experienced? I know who I would rather be.

We have both agreed that we would be very keen to do such an adventure together again in the future. The planning can only start once the hard part of deciding where we want to explore is complete. Let the endless fantasising of possible escapades begin.

There was talk, during the rally, we would ride motorbikes through Mongolia from Ulaanbaatar and around the Pamir Highway to complete what we had missed. We will have to come up with a way to achieve a happy medium, where both time and money are satisfied.

Appendix i: The Charities

The third of the only three rules that are imposed by the Adventurists for the Mongol rally, is that each team must raise over £1000 for charity. £500 of this must go to Cool Earth, their regular charity, and the rest can be donated to charities of your own choosing.

The reason we chose our charities is probably best summed up by the interviews Mikey and Max Levene gave for Rugby World magazine. The article was published in the magazine to help give our fundraising some more exposure before we set off.

"Mike Parlby and Ed Blackwell will hit the road in a 0.8 litre Daewoo Matiz – all Mongol Rally cars must be under one litre – and they'll set off from the UK on 16 July, hoping to reach the finish in Siberia within their five-week target or by the 12 September deadline.

They need to raise a minimum of £1,000 to take part – money which will then be split between the organisers' favoured rainforest charity, Cool Earth, and Parlby and Blackwell's chosen charities, the Max Levene Trust, and Back Up, which helps people in the UK who have spinal injuries.

The duo were playing for Kelly College against Truro School in 2009 when 17-year-old Truro player Levene suffered his spinal injury. 'I was on the other pitch but Ed was in his game. When it happened, both games stopped and everyone was aware of what was going on,' recalls Parlby.

Truro School set up the trust to help Max with the slogan 'Remember the boy, support the man' and thousands have since been raised by them and the local rugby community. Levene beat the odds to return to school and take his A Levels and he is currently finishing a Masters degree in development economics at the University of East Anglia. He says: 'The trust has been brilliant, allowing me to do lots of things I wouldn't have been able to do otherwise, and I think it's an honour that people still think about me and the accident.'

"See Ya Later Shit Lords!"

Despite his life-changing injury, Levene does not support recent calls for tackling to be banned in schools rugby. 'I feel it would completely kill the game at junior level. I don't think people should be forced to play contact rugby but we chose to play it and were coached to tackle properly.'"

The Back Up Trust

The Back Up Trust, or Back Up, is a UK charity which helps people of all ages and backgrounds rebuild their confidence and independence following a devastating spinal injury. Back Up were instrumental in Max's rehabilitation and continue to do fantastic work today.

A team of three paraplegics entered the rally in 2012, also in aid of this charity. It was tough for us, but I can't imagine what those guys went through. Especially as they picked a Rover 75, which broke down 500km from the finish meaning they had to take the Uaz 'bus' to UlanBataar. I take my hat off to them.

Further details of how Back Up change people's lives can be found at this website: www.backuptrust.org.uk/home

The Max Levene Trust

Max was a boarder at Truro School when he suffered a serious accident playing rugby for the school in October 2009 in a fixture against Kelly College. After the accident the school set up the trust with the slogan; 'Remember the boy, support the man'.

Over the years the trust has helped Max in many ways from helping to purchase adapted fitness equipment such as an FES exercise bike, to adapting a room at his Grandparents house so that he can continue to see his family.

Cool Earth

Half of the world's rainforest has been destroyed in the last 40 years. And, contrary to the headlines, rainforest continues to be lost at a faster rate than ever.

Cool Earth is the only charity that works solely where the threat to the forest is greatest, on the frontline of deforestation.

Their mission is to end the cycle of deforestation entrenching villages into further poverty through the creation of strong, self-determining communities – not dependency. Again, more information can be found at this website: www.coolearth.org

Appendix ii: The Sponsors

Fletcher's Solicitors

Fletcher's Solicitors are a law firm who specialise in serious injury, motorbike accidents, and medical negligence. They have a link with 'The Back Up Trust' which made them even more keen to get on board with this endeavour.

They were our main sponsors and kindly gave us a donation that put a huge dent in the ever increasing costs to actually get the trip off the ground in the first place. For example visas, car (admittedly not much), various essential gear. They wanted to use our adventure in one of their promotional videos, therefore they also gave us two Go-Pro cameras to make sure we didn't miss a shot. We returned with a mountain of footage and transferred it across (painstakingly on Dropbox) to Glued Films. They interviewed Mikey and myself bringing together the footage we filmed from the trip with the said interview to create a nice little edited summary video.

I have watched it countless times since it was finished as it evokes great memories of the adventure. Thanks again must go to these fantastic companies.

These are the links to Fletcher's and Glued Films websites:
www.fletcherssolicitors.co.uk
www.gluedfilms.com
The video is on our Facebook page: www.facebook.com/bataarlatethannever

Rotary Club International

The Rotary Club is a global network of 1.2 million neighbours, friends, leaders, and problem-solvers who come together to make positive, lasting change in communities at home and abroad.

Mikey's mum is the chairwoman of the Tavistock Club and was keen to get the word of the Rotary Club out there. We adorned Dominique with as many of the Rotary stickers as we could. Even the petrol filling cap.

We also took a list of the international Rotary Clubs that would be on our route. Unfortunately we didn't have an opportunity to drop into any, but it does make you realise how much of the world is covered by these absolute heroes who are there to help out the rest of their community. The link to their website is below:

www.rotary.org

Graspan Frankton

These guys also helped hugely with sponsorship, and we gave them advertising space on Dominique in return. However their logo provided a bit of a worry when traversing famous military heavy countries such as Russia, as you will see if you check out their website from the link below. They are a Newcastle based security company, looking to provide protection for companies in all sorts of industries.

www.graspanfrankton.com

Milford Farm

This is my girlfriend, Lottie's, family business, they are a turkey producer and wholesale meat supplier. They gave us the contact for John Earp, who made sure Dominique was fighting fit and would not break down before Dover. They also bought us many various tools and equipment that proved to be vital.

www.milfordfarm.co.uk

GoFilmYourself

These guys are a small start-up business, based in Newcastle. They rent out GoPro cameras on a daily/weekly basis. They kindly lent us a GoPro camera and all of the various mounts we would need to capture footage throughout the trip.

www.gofilmyourself.com

Polyflor

Polyflor are a leading international supplier of a variety of different types of floors. They were kind enough to donate to our

"See Ya Later Shit Lords!"

charities, and in return we plastered on the stickers to the car as well as wearing our donated polyflor t-shirts with pride. The link is below:

www.polyflor.co.uk

Advanced Engravers

This is a recently new company that had only just formed as we were setting off. The founder, a friend of mine, sorted us out ten boxes of 24 hour ration packs. These turned out to be one of the most important pre packed items we took. The bag they were packed in got lighter, the closer and more worn out, the car became. They also saved our bacon in Bulgaria.

Anyway, this is a fantastic Newcastle based company, who deliver to the UK, for all your engraving needs. You have to be careful though, if you stay still around Mick too long he may engrave a logo on to you. Link below:

www.advancedengravers.co.uk/

Appendix iii: Dos and Don'ts

Do:

- Buy a Daewoo Matiz
- Get someone who knows what they're doing to check over the car before you leave.
- Take lots of pictures, because you never know who's going to steal them/lose them.
- Take spare parts – the ones we took saved our bacon.
- Try and find a river to wash in when facilities are scarce. It will be the best washing experience you have. Austrian variety recommended.
- Plan more time than your first estimate. Recommend adding at least two weeks of contingency.
- Pay to drive around the Nurburgring. Incredible experience.
- Try to sleep in hammocks as frequently as possible. You can thank me later for that piece of advice.
- Take advice from locals – although maybe not about angle grinding in a straw house.
- Make tallies of various reoccurring events on the trip – flat tyre chart.
- Try to see as many capitals as possible, you never know when they might come up in a pub quiz.
- Frequently repack the car when you can.
- Prepare to add 20% of your original budget.
- Always make time for other ralliers, stop whenever you see the infamous red stickers.
- Get someone who knows Russian to write a note saying that you have run out of money.
- Enjoy everything you are doing at the time.

"See Ya Later Shit Lords!"

Don't:
- Be surprised when you have to fork out three times the amount you paid for the car to fix it.
- Buy a Peugeot 205 (or a car with torsion bar suspension)
- Let more than one border guard go through your car at once. They are bastards and they will steal anything they can. This is only really Turkmenistan, the others were good.
- Book flights until you at least two thirds of the way through your trip and you have a really good estimate of where you will be at certain dates. We regrettably had to miss bits because of this.
- Ever pay a police fine when they pull you over in a country ending in -stan.
- Think you will stick exactly to the route you originally planned in your bedroom.
- Believe it takes just three days to cross the Pamir Highway.
- Be shocked when your preconceptions of a place are shattered, be it for positive or negative.
- Forget your 'When the shit hits the fan' bag, very useful for Henry and Frosty.
- Go on the trip with people you met on the internet. Make sure you actually like your companion, otherwise it is going to be a long trip.
- Let anyone hold your passport when it is out of your sight.
- Forget to pay post rally fines. They will find you in the UK.
- Turn down WiFi or a chance to wash, be it a river or shower.
- Be afraid to bribe the right people. No shame.
- Be put off by recent world events – for example the military coup in Turkey, it was just a classic coup.

"See Ya Later Shit Lords!"
Appendix iv: The Route

This was the exact text we had written on the inside of Dominique's roof. We started with the UK just above our heads in the front and by the end we were having to crawl to the back of the car to notch up Russia. There is a couple of words summing up each country and the date was only allowed to be written up on the day we left the country.

Russia - 20/08/16 (Fin)
Kazakhstan – 17/08/16 (Dollar)
Kyrgyzstan – 15/08/16 (MISHA)
Tajikistan – 13/08/16 (Broken)
Uzbekistan – 09/08/16 (Chipa)
Turkmenistan – 07/08/16 (Cunts)
Azerbaijan - 04/08/16 (Even longer)
Georgia – 29/07/16 (Lucky, Lucky)
Turkey – 27/07/16 (Surprisingly Good)
Romania – 23/07/16 (Hungover)
Bulgaria – 22/07/16 (Shit Day)
Serbia – 21/07/16 (Fucking Long)
Hungary – 21/07/16 (HUF)
Slovenia – 20/07/16 (Brief)
Austria – 20/07/16 (Idyllic)
Germany – 19/07/16 (Ausfahrt)
Netherlands – 18/07/16 (Wash 1)
Belgium – 18/07/16 (Mildly Followed)
France – 17/08/16 (UNTERWEG)
UK – 17/08/16 (Commence)

"See Ya Later Shit Lords!"

"See Ya Later Shit Lords!"
Appendix v: Kit List

Car Parts and Tools		
Item	**Used?**	**Comments**
Car	Yes	Less than 1 litre engine
V5C	Yes	Won't get through any borders east of Europe without it. Vital
Spare wheels	Frequently	Became an ever-changing part of our car. Got through over 10.
Sump guard	Yes	Removed after car was killed in Pamirs. Started to knock on the gearbox.
Roof bars	Yes	Held on roofbox
Roof box	Yes	Barely clinging on by the end
Spare rear suspension arm	No	Needed it just in case.
Spare front suspension arm	Very much so	Resurrected Dominique in the Pamirs
Spare suspension springs	No	Picked up some spares in Kazakhstan.
Air filters	Changed once	After dusty roads
Fuel filters	Never	Might have needed changing
Fuel funnel	Yes	Used every time we filled up from jerry cans.
Socket and spanner set	Yes (especially 17mm variety)	Lost most of the set through the holes in the roofbox

"See Ya Later Shit Lords!"

Screwdrivers	Not really	Multi-tool covered most
Multi-tool	Yes	Very handy
Tyre pump	No	Generally the tyres were so fucked the guys at the garage would have to replace the whole wheel.
Belts for alternator and power steering	Yes	Picked up along the way.
Two massive extra headlamps wired up to the full beam	Very much	These were fantastic. The original lights were very poor so our main beam was a God send.
Car jack	A lot	Every time we changed a tyre.
Axle stands	Useful	Very dangerous to go under a car just on jacks. We took the Pug crawlers once they had to bow out.
Ratchet straps	Yes	Pretty much held the roofbox on by the end
Rope	Yes	Used for the tarpaulin over the hammocks as well as towing.
Grease	No	Worth having though.
2 x Jerry cans	Yes	These are vital. Served as our back up fuel reserve. Don't keep inside the vehicle, although we think these were the downfall of the roofbox. Also some countries don't allow jerry cans to be full.

"See Ya Later Shit Lords!"

20L Water container	Yes	Mikey was always very reassured when the tank was brimmed.
Spade	Yes	Used for digging a shit hole as well as trying to dig out Dominique in Russia. Although a massive Russian truck does the trick as well.
WD40	Yes	Keeps things moving, vital for any engineering.
Duct Tape	Yes	Stops things from moving, vital for any engineering.
Hammer	Yes	Useful when peeling the wheel arches when we had oversized tyres.
Axe	Never	Wouldn't go without one. You never know what might happen
Hi-Vis Jacket	Never	Needed, as part of the law, for the 30 minutes of driving in France.
Warning triangle	Never	Needed, as part of the law, for the 30 minutes of driving in France.
12V Dual adapter	Yes	Very useful, kept everything charged throughout the trip. Would maybe opt for an inverter next time.
12V Aux cable	Yes	Connects to the radio, through frequency, to allow own tunes to be played. Did often get interference from local stations.

"See Ya Later Shit Lords!"

Radio	Yes	Fried the charger with first use so rarely used after.
Maps for all the countries	Sort of	Never actually really used, Maps.me was used on our phones instead. Beware of this evil mistress though.

Camping and Personal Equipment

Item	Used?	Comments
Passport	Yes	Every border.
Travel insurance	Yes	Make sure you have it.
Visas	Yes	Sort all of these out before you go otherwise your trip will be cut very short.
Money	Yes	Just get lots of euros and dollars but don't lose/have them stolen like both of us.
Hammocks	Yes	Pretty much every night we camped.
Tarpaulin	Yes	When it looked like it was going to rain.
Tent	Bitterly	Used on the rare occasion when we couldn't/were too tired to find anchor points for hammocks.
Sleeping Bag	Yes	Every camping night.
Pillow	Yes	Very grim looking by the end.
Toilet paper	Yes	For nature toilets
Collapsible Toilet Seat	Mikey mainly	See Chapter 'Mother Russia' for hilarious mishap.
Stove	Yes	Used for cooking boil-in-the-bags.
Travel 12V kettle, coffee, cafetiere, and insulated travel mug.	Everyday	Vital to awake Mikey every morning
Lighter	Yes	Used for obvious reasons.
Torches	Yes	Needed for all the night driving we weren't planning on doing.
Camping lantern	Yes	Useful in the tent.
Matches	Yes	For when the lighters were lost.

"See Ya Later Shit Lords!"

Knife	Yes	I bought Mikey a massive Russian knife in a service station. It wasn't to be messed with.
12V Coolbox/refrigerator	Yes	This was really good at keeping stuff at a medium temperature. Because it was so hot in the car the machine had to work overtime and often hindered other charging.
Camping Chairs	Yes	At every campsite. The best place was on the Pamir highway.
Bin bags	Yes	Essential for leaving nothing but footprints.
Extra blanket	No	Never really got cold enough.
First aid kit	Yes	Ours was in a plastic box. Essential for all potential eventualities.
Sun cream	Yes	Especially for the arm that was hanging out the window. Stopped trucker tans.
After sun	Yes	Used for when the above was forgotten about.
Mosquito repellent	Yes	A layer was often sprayed around the hammocks before the night. Be careful not to spray too much as apparently that attracts them.
10 x 24hr Ration Packs	Yes	Saved our lives on more than one occasion.
General long lasting food	Yes	Nibbled on these throughout the journey.
Camping showers	Part of	The hose became highly useful when bodging a fuel filling issue in the Pug. Never actually used

"See Ya Later Shit Lords!"

		them for their function, we preferred washing as God intended.
Sunglasses	Yes	Almost never taken off
FlipFlops	Yes	No other shoes were worn by either of us, we drove in bare feet, for the whole trip apart from when I drove around the Nurburging.
Clothes	Yes	Mainly t-shirts and shorts. Few essential layers just in case it got colder in the night.

I am sure that this list was much more extensive as the car seemed to be permanently full to bursting. But I can't seem to remember any more, it probably was never used if it was in the car and I have forgotten it.

"See Ya Later Shit Lords!"
Appendix vi: Currency Conversions

This section will hopefully give you some idea of how much we were paying for things in the countries with currencies you do not recognise. This should be correct from the 16th July 2016 (the date we left) however this will have wildly changed now, thanks to Brexit.

	Units Per GBP	
USD	US Dollar	1.32
EUR	Euro	1.19
HUF	Hungarian Forint	377.20
BGN	Bulgarian Lev	2.33
GEL	Georgian Lari	3.09
AZN	Azerbaijani New Manat	2.05
KZT	Kazakhstani Tenge	447.30
KGS	Kyrgyzstani Som	88.68
MZN	Mongolian Tughrik	2641.24
RUB	Russian Ruble	83.61
RSD	Serbian Dinar	145.72
TJS	Tajikistani Somoni	10.37
TMT	Turkmenistani Manat	4.62
UZS	Uzbekistani Som	3924.92
TRY	Turkish Lira	3.98
RON	Romanian New Leu	5.34

Printed in Great Britain
by Amazon